The International
Sailing Logbook
by Steve Colgate

This book belongs to: _____

Address: _____

City/State/Zip: _____

Phone: _____

About the Author

Steve Colgate is the author of numerous books and articles on sailing. He and his wife Doris own Offshore Sailing School Ltd., one of the oldest, largest and most reputable sailing schools in the U.S. Over the years Steve has sailed in 6 Trans-Atlantic Races, 8 Bermuda Races, 2 America's Cup trials, Pan-American Games, 1968 Olympics, Sydney-Hobart Race and numerous other races and cruises. Because of Steve's reputation as the leading sailing educator in the country, the United States Yacht Racing Union (USYRU) appointed him to their Training Committee to help develop standards for the certification of sailing instructors, thus insuring a positive and safe experience for those taking a sailing course.

Library of Congress Catalog Card Number: 83-062708
ISBN: 0-914747-00-2 / Printed in the United States of America
Published by Offshore Sailing School Ltd.
190 East Schofield Street, City Island, New York 10464 / Phone: (212) 885-3200

Preface

The purpose of this log is to enable every sailor to keep an easily verifiable record of his or her sailing experience and courses taken. Your sailing experience can be verified by the director of any school and any charter agency or any private owner or charterboat. While schools and charter agencies vary in quality, nothing can replace the experience of on-the-water practice. This book is divided into three sections followed by useful appendicies.

Section One/Courses Taken: In this section list all the various sailing, navigation, CPR, First Aid, Coast Guard, and other boating safety courses you have taken, and have each certified by the highest level person involved with the course or school.

Section Two/Sailing Log: Here you can list all the sailing charters, rentals, cruises and races you have participated in. Have them verified by the charter agency, the boat's skipper or by crew if you own your own boat.

Section Three/Sailing Tests: Though this log is primarily a record of your sailing experience, this section lists the minimum standards necessary for the various levels of sailing proficiency. Knowledge of each item can be verified by a qualified person after testing. Most large sailing schools will have an instructor who is qualified to check you out on the items in this section. If he or she works for Offshore Sailing School or, if not, has been trained and certified by the USYRU—the only nationally recognized non-profit sailing authority in the United States, founded in 1897—you can be absolutely positive that your instructor has sufficient level of experience to verify your knowledge.

Appendices: The last section lists many more important navigation rules, distress signals and chart symbols. They are a handy reference when underway whether sailing or powering.

Section One:
Courses Taken

School or Organization's Name: Offshore Sailing School Ltd.	School or Organization's Name:
Address: 16731-110 McGregor Blvd.	Address:
City/State/Zip: Ft. Myers, FL 33908	City/State/Zip:
Phone: 813-454-1700	Phone:
Course Title: LIVE ABOARD CRUISING	Course Title:
Course Description: BARE BOAT CERTIFICATION	Course Description:
Date of Course: 6/11 - 6/18/89	Date of Course:
Location of Course: ST LUCIA BWI	Location of Course:
Class of Boat: MOORINGS 43	Class of Boat:
Size, Rig & Type: 43' AUX SLOOP	Size, Rig & Type:
Number of Hours on Water: 6 DAYS	Number of Hours on Water:
Number of Hours in Classroom: O	Number of Hours in Classroom:
Below to Be Filled Out by Certifier	**Below to Be Filled Out by Certifier**
Rating (Fail, Pass, High Pass, Outstanding):	Rating (Fail, Pass, High Pass, Outstanding):
Certifier's Signature:	Certifier's Signature:
Certifier's Name (Print): TYLER PIERCE	Certifier's Name (Print):
Certifier's Position: DIRECTOR OF OPERATIONS	Certifier's Position:
Credentials (Years Sailed, Licenses, Etc.):	Credentials (Years Sailed, Licenses, Etc.):
Certifier's Address: Offshore Sailing School Ltd. 16731-110 McGregor Blvd.	Certifier's Address:
City/State/Zip: Ft. Myers, FL 33908	City/State/Zip:
Phone: 813-454-1700	Phone:
Notes:	Notes:

School or Organization's Name:

Address:

City/State/Zip:

Phone:

Course Title:

Course Description:

Date of Course:

Location of Course:

Class of Boat:

Size, Rig & Type:

Number of Hours on Water:

Number of Hours in Classroom:

Below to Be Filled Out by Certifier

Rating (Fail, Pass, High Pass, Outstanding):

Certifier's Signature:

Certifier's Name (Print):

Certifier's Position:

Credentials (Years Sailed, Licenses, Etc.):

Certifier's Address:

City/State/Zip:

Phone:

Notes:

School or Organization's Name:

Address:

City/State/Zip:

Phone:

Course Title:

Course Description:

Date of Course:

Location of Course:

Class of Boat:

Size, Rig & Type:

Number of Hours on Water:

Number of Hours in Classroom:

Below to Be Filled Out by Certifier

Rating (Fail, Pass, High Pass, Outstanding):

Certifier's Signature:

Certifier's Name (Print):

Certifier's Position:

Credentials (Years Sailed, Licenses, Etc.):

Certifier's Address:

City/State/Zip:

Phone:

Notes:

School or Organization's Name:	School or Organization's Name:
Address:	Address:
City/State/Zip:	City/State/Zip:
Phone:	Phone:
Course Title:	Course Title:
Course Description:	Course Description:
Date of Course:	Date of Course:
Location of Course:	Location of Course:
Class of Boat:	Class of Boat:
Size, Rig & Type:	Size, Rig & Type:
Number of Hours on Water:	Number of Hours on Water:
Number of Hours in Classroom:	Number of Hours in Classroom:

Below to Be Filled Out by Certifier	**Below to Be Filled Out by Certifier**
Rating (Fail, Pass, High Pass, Outstanding):	Rating (Fail, Pass, High Pass, Outstanding):
Certifier's Signature:	Certifier's Signature:
Certifier's Name (Print):	Certifier's Name (Print):
Certifier's Position:	Certifier's Position:
Credentials (Years Sailed, Licenses, Etc.):	Credentials (Years Sailed, Licenses, Etc.):
Certifier's Address:	Certifier's Address:
City/State/Zip:	City/State/Zip:
Phone:	Phone:
Notes:	Notes:

School or Organization's Name:

Address:

City/State/Zip:

Phone:

Course Title:

Course Description:

Date of Course:

Location of Course:

Class of Boat:

Size, Rig & Type:

Number of Hours on Water:

Number of Hours in Classroom:

Below to Be Filled Out by Certifier

Rating (Fail, Pass, High Pass, Outstanding):

Certifier's Signature:

Certifier's Name (Print):

Certifier's Position:

Credentials (Years Sailed, Licenses, Etc.):

Certifier's Address:

City/State/Zip:

Phone:

Notes:

School or Organization's Name:

Address:

City/State/Zip:

Phone:

Course Title:

Course Description:

Date of Course:

Location of Course:

Class of Boat:

Size, Rig & Type:

Number of Hours on Water:

Number of Hours in Classroom:

Below to Be Filled Out by Certifier

Rating (Fail, Pass, High Pass, Outstanding):

Certifier's Signature:

Certifier's Name (Print):

Certifier's Position:

Credentials (Years Sailed, Licenses, Etc.):

Certifier's Address:

City/State/Zip:

Phone:

Notes:

School or Organization's Name:

Address:

City/State/Zip:

Phone:

Course Title:

Course Description:

Date of Course:

Location of Course:

Class of Boat:

Size, Rig & Type:

Number of Hours on Water:

Number of Hours in Classroom:

Below to Be Filled Out by Certifier

Rating (Fail, Pass, High Pass, Outstanding):

Certifier's Signature:

Certifier's Name (Print):

Certifier's Position:

Credentials (Years Sailed, Licenses, Etc.):

Certifier's Address:

City/State/Zip:

Phone:

Notes:

School or Organization's Name:

Address:

City/State/Zip:

Phone:

Course Title:

Course Description:

Date of Course:

Location of Course:

Class of Boat:

Size, Rig & Type:

Number of Hours on Water:

Number of Hours in Classroom:

Below to Be Filled Out by Certifier

Rating (Fail, Pass, High Pass, Outstanding):

Certifier's Signature:

Certifier's Name (Print):

Certifier's Position:

Credentials (Years Sailed, Licenses, Etc.):

Certifier's Address:

City/State/Zip:

Phone:

Notes:

School or Organization's Name:

Address:

City/State/Zip:

Phone:

Course Title:

Course Description:

Date of Course:

Location of Course:

Class of Boat:

Size, Rig & Type:

Number of Hours on Water:

Number of Hours in Classroom:

Below to Be Filled Out by Certifier

Rating (Fail, Pass, High Pass, Outstanding):

Certifier's Signature:

Certifier's Name (Print):

Certifier's Position:

Credentials (Years Sailed, Licenses, Etc.):

Certifier's Address:

City/State/Zip:

Phone:

Notes:

School or Organization's Name:

Address:

City/State/Zip:

Phone:

Course Title:

Course Description:

Date of Course:

Location of Course:

Class of Boat:

Size, Rig & Type:

Number of Hours on Water:

Number of Hours in Classroom:

Below to Be Filled Out by Certifier

Rating (Fail, Pass, High Pass, Outstanding):

Certifier's Signature:

Certifier's Name (Print):

Certifier's Position:

Credentials (Years Sailed, Licenses, Etc.):

Certifier's Address:

City/State/Zip:

Phone:

Notes:

Section Two:
The Sailing Log

The following Sailing Log is of special interest to those who may want to record their experience in order to obtain a U.S. Coast Guard license.

A Coast Guard license is required for anyone who carries passengers for hire on a motorboat in U.S. waters. Legally, the meaning of "for hire" has become very broad. Money doesn't have to change hands if there is another form of remuneration. It applies to charterers, sailing instructors, taking out business clients, and even guests who share expenses with the owner. A sailboat is a motorboat under these rules if it has an engine, whether or not it is in use. Even a small daysailer with an outboard motor is a motorboat and needs a licensed captain if it is being used for business. A Coast Guard license is not required if the boat does not have an engine and the operator is not carrying more than six persons for hire.

There are many levels of Coast Guard licenses, but the one that has the most universal application is the "Motorboat Operators" license. It is covered in the U.S. Coast Guard's Title 46—Subpart 10.20, and is for licensing applicants to operate motorboats of 15 gross tons or less while carrying six or less passengers for hire. Applicants must [a] be at least 18 years old, [b] submit evidence of at least 365 days experience in the operation of motorboats, [c] speak, read and understand English, [d] have not been convicted of a violation of drug law, [e] take a Coast Guard examination, [f] be physically fit, [g] have uncorrected vision of at least 20/100 in both eyes correctable to at least 20/20 in one eye and 20/40 in the other and [h] not be color blind.

Of these requirements, the two most difficult for many sailors are the proof of 365 days experience and passing the Coast Guard examination.

This log will help you establish this record. When you have enough time logged, obtain the Coast Guard "Certification of Service" forms, fill them out and send them to your certifiers for their signature and the required notarization. You can even send them a copy of the page they signed in your log, so they don't have to check their records.

Help on the second problem, the examination, can be obtained through one of the firms that prepares candidates for the exam. Some offer correspondence/home-study courses. Others give classroom courses. A partial list appears on the insert in the back of this log.

Record of
Cruises, Deliveries, Etc.

Trip:	1	2	3
Date:			
Location:			
From:			
To:			
Average Miles from Shore:			
Maximum Miles from Shore:			
Boat Name:			
Boat Type & Rig:			
Documentation or Reg. No.:			
Length:			
Gross Tons:			
Engine Horsepower:			
Type of Sailing Done:*			
Position on Boat:**			
Boat Ownership:***			
Certifier's Signature:			
Certifier's Name (Print):			
Certifier's Position:			
Certifier's Street Address:			
Certifier's City/State/Zip:			
Certifier's Phone Number:			

Legend: *Sailing Done: [D] Daysailing, [C] Cruising, [R] Racing. **Position: [S] Skipper, [M] Mate, [N] Navigator, [C] Crew. ***Ownership: [R] Rental Daysailer, [B] Bareboat Cruising, [C] Crewed Cruising, [F] Friend's Boat, [O] Own Boat.

Trip:	4	5	6
Date:			
Location:			
From:			
To:			
Average Miles from Shore:			
Maximum Miles from Shore:			
Boat Name:			
Boat Type & Rig:			
Documentation or Reg. No.:			
Length:			
Gross Tons:			
Engine Horsepower:			
Type of Sailing Done:*			
Position on Boat:**			
Boat Ownership:***			
Certifier's Signature:			
Certifier's Name (Print):			
Certifier's Position:			
Certifier's Street Address:			
Certifier's City/State/Zip:			
Certifier's Phone Number:			

Legend: *Sailing Done: [D] Daysailing, [C] Cruising, [R] Racing.

**Position: [S] Skipper, [M] Mate, [N] Navigator, [C] Crew.

***Ownership: [R] Rental Daysailer, [B] Bareboat Cruising, [C] Crewed Cruising,

[F] Friend's Boat, [O] Own Boat.

Notes:

Trip:	7	8	9
Date:			
Location:			
From:			
To:			
Average Miles from Shore:			
Maximum Miles from Shore:			
Boat Name:			
Boat Type & Rig:			
Documentation or Reg. No.:			
Length:			
Gross Tons:			
Engine Horsepower:			
Type of Sailing Done:*			
Position on Boat:**			
Boat Ownership:***			
Certifier's Signature:			
Certifier's Name (Print):			
Certifier's Position:			
Certifier's Street Address:			
Certifier's City/State/Zip:			
Certifier's Phone Number:			

Legend: *Sailing Done: [D] Daysailing, [C] Cruising, [R] Racing.

**Position: [S] Skipper, [M] Mate, [N] Navigator, [C] Crew.

***Ownership: [R] Rental Daysailer, [B] Bareboat Cruising, [C] Crewed Cruising,

[F] Friend's Boat, [O] Own Boat.

Notes:

Trip:	10	11	12
Date:			
Location:			
From:			
To:			
Average Miles from Shore:			
Maximum Miles from Shore:			
Boat Name:			
Boat Type & Rig:			
Documentation or Reg. No.:			
Length:			
Gross Tons:			
Engine Horsepower:			
Type of Sailing Done:*			
Position on Boat:**			
Boat Ownership:***			
Certifier's Signature:			
Certifier's Name (Print):			
Certifier's Position:			
Certifier's Street Address:			
Certifier's City/State/Zip:			
Certifier's Phone Number:			

Legend: *Sailing Done: [D] Daysailing, [C] Cruising, [R] Racing.

**Position: [S] Skipper, [M] Mate, [N] Navigator, [C] Crew.

***Ownership: [R] Rental Daysailer, [B] Bareboat Cruising, [C] Crewed Cruising,

[F] Friend's Boat, [O] Own Boat.

Notes:

Trip:	13	14	15
Date:			
Location:			
From:			
To:			
Average Miles from Shore:			
Maximum Miles from Shore:			
Boat Name:			
Boat Type & Rig:			
Documentation or Reg. No.:			
Length:			
Gross Tons:			
Engine Horsepower:			
Type of Sailing Done:*			
Position on Boat:**			
Boat Ownership:***			
Certifier's Signature:			
Certifier's Name (Print):			
Certifier's Position:			
Certifier's Street Address:			
Certifier's City/State/Zip:			
Certifier's Phone Number:			

Legend: *Sailing Done: [D] Daysailing, [C] Cruising, [R] Racing.

**Position: [S] Skipper, [M] Mate, [N] Navigator, [C] Crew.

***Ownership: [R] Rental Daysailer, [B] Bareboat Cruising, [C] Crewed Cruising,

[F] Friend's Boat, [O] Own Boat.

Notes:

Trip:	16	17	18
Date:			
Location:			
From:			
To:			
Average Miles from Shore:			
Maximum Miles from Shore:			
Boat Name:			
Boat Type & Rig:			
Documentation or Reg. No.:			
Length:			
Gross Tons:			
Engine Horsepower:			
Type of Sailing Done:*			
Position on Boat:**			
Boat Ownership:***			
Certifier's Signature:			
Certifier's Name (Print):			
Certifier's Position:			
Certifier's Street Address:			
Certifier's City/State/Zip:			
Certifier's Phone Number:			

Legend: *Sailing Done: [D] Daysailing, [C] Cruising, [R] Racing.

**Position: [S] Skipper, [M] Mate, [N] Navigator, [C] Crew.

***Ownership: [R] Rental Daysailer, [B] Bareboat Cruising, [C] Crewed Cruising,

[F] Friend's Boat, [O] Own Boat.

Notes:

Trip:	19	20	21
Date:			
Location:			
From:			
To:			
Average Miles from Shore:			
Maximum Miles from Shore:			
Boat Name:			
Boat Type & Rig:			
Documentation or Reg. No.:			
Length:			
Gross Tons:			
Engine Horsepower:			
Type of Sailing Done:*			
Position on Boat:**			
Boat Ownership:***			
Certifier's Signature:			
Certifier's Name (Print):			
Certifier's Position:			
Certifier's Street Address:			
Certifier's City/State/Zip:			
Certifier's Phone Number:			

Legend: *Sailing Done: [D] Daysailing, [C] Cruising, [R] Racing.

**Position: [S] Skipper, [M] Mate, [N] Navigator, [C] Crew.

***Ownership: [R] Rental Daysailer, [B] Bareboat Cruising, [C] Crewed Cruising,

[F] Friend's Boat, [O] Own Boat.

Notes:

Trip:	22	23	24
Date:			
Location:			
From:			
To:			
Average Miles from Shore:			
Maximum Miles from Shore:			
Boat Name:			
Boat Type & Rig:			
Documentation or Reg. No.:			
Length:			
Gross Tons:			
Engine Horsepower:			
Type of Sailing Done:*			
Position on Boat:**			
Boat Ownership:***			
Certifier's Signature:			
Certifier's Name (Print):			
Certifier's Position:			
Certifier's Street Address:			
Certifier's City/State/Zip:			
Certifier's Phone Number:			

Legend: *Sailing Done: [D] Daysailing, [C] Cruising, [R] Racing.

**Position: [S] Skipper, [M] Mate, [N] Navigator, [C] Crew.

***Ownership: [R] Rental Daysailer, [B] Bareboat Cruising, [C] Crewed Cruising,

[F] Friend's Boat, [O] Own Boat.

Notes:

Trip:	25	26	27
Date:			
Location:			
From:			
To:			
Average Miles from Shore:			
Maximum Miles from Shore:			
Boat Name:			
Boat Type & Rig:			
Documentation or Reg. No.:			
Length:			
Gross Tons:			
Engine Horsepower:			
Type of Sailing Done:*			
Position on Boat:**			
Boat Ownership:***			
Certifier's Signature:			
Certifier's Name (Print):			
Certifier's Position:			
Certifier's Street Address:			
Certifier's City/State/Zip:			
Certifier's Phone Number:			

Legend: *Sailing Done: [D] Daysailing, [C] Cruising, [R] Racing.

**Position: [S] Skipper, [M] Mate, [N] Navigator, [C] Crew.

***Ownership: [R] Rental Daysailer, [B] Bareboat Cruising, [C] Crewed Cruising,

[F] Friend's Boat, [O] Own Boat.

Notes:

Trip:	28	29	30
Date:			
Location:			
From:			
To:			
Average Miles from Shore:			
Maximum Miles from Shore:			
Boat Name:			
Boat Type & Rig:			
Documentation or Reg. No.:			
Length:			
Gross Tons:			
Engine Horsepower:			
Type of Sailing Done:*			
Position on Boat:**			
Boat Ownership:***			
Certifier's Signature:			
Certifier's Name (Print):			
Certifier's Position:			
Certifier's Street Address:			
Certifier's City/State/Zip:			
Certifier's Phone Number:			

Legend: *Sailing Done: [D] Daysailing, [C] Cruising, [R] Racing.

**Position: [S] Skipper, [M] Mate, [N] Navigator, [C] Crew.

***Ownership: [R] Rental Daysailer, [B] Bareboat Cruising, [C] Crewed Cruising,

[F] Friend's Boat, [O] Own Boat.

Notes:

Trip:	31	32	33
Date:			
Location:			
From:			
To:			
Average Miles from Shore:			
Maximum Miles from Shore:			
Boat Name:			
Boat Type & Rig:			
Documentation or Reg. No.:			
Length:			
Gross Tons:			
Engine Horsepower:			
Type of Sailing Done:*			
Position on Boat:**			
Boat Ownership:***			
Certifier's Signature:			
Certifier's Name (Print):			
Certifier's Position:			
Certifier's Street Address:			
Certifier's City/State/Zip:			
Certifier's Phone Number:			

Legend: *Sailing Done: [D] Daysailing, [C] Cruising, [R] Racing.

**Position: [S] Skipper, [M] Mate, [N] Navigator, [C] Crew.

***Ownership: [R] Rental Daysailer, [B] Bareboat Cruising, [C] Crewed Cruising,

[F] Friend's Boat, [O] Own Boat.

Notes:

Trip:	34	35	36
Date:			
Location:			
From:			
To:			
Average Miles from Shore:			
Maximum Miles from Shore:			
Boat Name:			
Boat Type & Rig:			
Documentation or Reg. No.:			
Length:			
Gross Tons:			
Engine Horsepower:			
Type of Sailing Done:*			
Position on Boat:**			
Boat Ownership:***			
Certifier's Signature:			
Certifier's Name (Print):			
Certifier's Position:			
Certifier's Street Address:			
Certifier's City/State/Zip:			
Certifier's Phone Number:			

Legend: *Sailing Done: [D] Daysailing, [C] Cruising, [R] Racing.

**Position: [S] Skipper, [M] Mate, [N] Navigator, [C] Crew.

***Ownership: [R] Rental Daysailer, [B] Bareboat Cruising, [C] Crewed Cruising,

[F] Friend's Boat, [O] Own Boat.

Notes:

Trip:	37	38	39
Date:			
Location:			
From:			
To:			
Average Miles from Shore:			
Maximum Miles from Shore:			
Boat Name:			
Boat Type & Rig:			
Documentation or Reg. No.:			
Length:			
Gross Tons:			
Engine Horsepower:			
Type of Sailing Done:*			
Position on Boat:**			
Boat Ownership:***			
Certifier's Signature:			
Certifier's Name (Print):			
Certifier's Position:			
Certifier's Street Address:			
Certifier's City/State/Zip:			
Certifier's Phone Number:			

Legend: *Sailing Done: [D] Daysailing, [C] Cruising, [R] Racing.

**Position: [S] Skipper, [M] Mate, [N] Navigator, [C] Crew.

***Ownership: [R] Rental Daysailer, [B] Bareboat Cruising, [C] Crewed Cruising,

[F] Friend's Boat, [O] Own Boat.

Notes:

Trip:	40	41	42
Date:			
Location:			
From:			
To:			
Average Miles from Shore:			
Maximum Miles from Shore:			
Boat Name:			
Boat Type & Rig:			
Documentation or Reg. No.:			
Length:			
Gross Tons:			
Engine Horsepower:			
Type of Sailing Done:*			
Position on Boat:**			
Boat Ownership:***			
Certifier's Signature:			
Certifier's Name (Print):			
Certifier's Position:			
Certifier's Street Address:			
Certifier's City/State/Zip:			
Certifier's Phone Number:			

Legend: *Sailing Done: [D] Daysailing, [C] Cruising, [R] Racing.

**Position: [S] Skipper, [M] Mate, [N] Navigator, [C] Crew.

***Ownership: [R] Rental Daysailer, [B] Bareboat Cruising, [C] Crewed Cruising,

[F] Friend's Boat, [O] Own Boat.

Notes:

Trip:	43	44	45
Date:			
Location:			
From:			
To:			
Average Miles from Shore:			
Maximum Miles from Shore:			
Boat Name:			
Boat Type & Rig:			
Documentation or Reg. No.:			
Length:			
Gross Tons:			
Engine Horsepower:			
Type of Sailing Done:*			
Position on Boat:**			
Boat Ownership:***			
Certifier's Signature:			
Certifier's Name (Print):			
Certifier's Position:			
Certifier's Street Address:			
Certifier's City/State/Zip:			
Certifier's Phone Number:			

Legend: *Sailing Done: [D] Daysailing, [C] Cruising, [R] Racing.

**Position: [S] Skipper, [M] Mate, [N] Navigator, [C] Crew.

***Ownership: [R] Rental Daysailer, [B] Bareboat Cruising, [C] Crewed Cruising,

[F] Friend's Boat, [O] Own Boat.

Notes:

Trip:	46	47	48
Date:			
Location:			
From:			
To:			
Average Miles from Shore:			
Maximum Miles from Shore:			
Boat Name:			
Boat Type & Rig:			
Documentation or Reg. No.:			
Length:			
Gross Tons:			
Engine Horsepower:			
Type of Sailing Done:*			
Position on Boat:**			
Boat Ownership:***			
Certifier's Signature:			
Certifier's Name (Print):			
Certifier's Position:			
Certifier's Street Address:			
Certifier's City/State/Zip:			
Certifier's Phone Number:			

Legend: *Sailing Done: [D] Daysailing, [C] Cruising, [R] Racing.

**Position: [S] Skipper, [M] Mate, [N] Navigator, [C] Crew.

***Ownership: [R] Rental Daysailer, [B] Bareboat Cruising, [C] Crewed Cruising,

[F] Friend's Boat, [O] Own Boat.

Notes:

Trip:	49	50	51
Date:			
Location:			
From:			
To:			
Average Miles from Shore:			
Maximum Miles from Shore:			
Boat Name:			
Boat Type & Rig:			
Documentation or Reg. No.:			
Length:			
Gross Tons:			
Engine Horsepower:			
Type of Sailing Done:*			
Position on Boat:**			
Boat Ownership:***			
Certifier's Signature:			
Certifier's Name (Print):			
Certifier's Position:			
Certifier's Street Address:			
Certifier's City/State/Zip:			
Certifier's Phone Number:			

Legend: *Sailing Done: [D] Daysailing, [C] Cruising, [R] Racing.

**Position: [S] Skipper, [M] Mate, [N] Navigator, [C] Crew.

***Ownership: [R] Rental Daysailer, [B] Bareboat Cruising, [C] Crewed Cruising,

[F] Friend's Boat, [O] Own Boat.

Notes:

Trip:	52	53	54
Date:			
Location:			
From:			
To:			
Average Miles from Shore:			
Maximum Miles from Shore:			
Boat Name:			
Boat Type & Rig:			
Documentation or Reg. No.:			
Length:			
Gross Tons:			
Engine Horsepower:			
Type of Sailing Done:*			
Position on Boat:**			
Boat Ownership:***			
Certifier's Signature:			
Certifier's Name (Print):			
Certifier's Position:			
Certifier's Street Address:			
Certifier's City/State/Zip:			
Certifier's Phone Number:			

Legend: *Sailing Done: [D] Daysailing, [C] Cruising, [R] Racing.

**Position: [S] Skipper, [M] Mate, [N] Navigator, [C] Crew.

***Ownership: [R] Rental Daysailer, [B] Bareboat Cruising, [C] Crewed Cruising,

[F] Friend's Boat, [O] Own Boat.

Notes:

Trip:	55	56	57
Date:			
Location:			
From:			
To:			
Average Miles from Shore:			
Maximum Miles from Shore:			
Boat Name:			
Boat Type & Rig:			
Documentation or Reg. No.:			
Length:			
Gross Tons:			
Engine Horsepower:			
Type of Sailing Done:*			
Position on Boat:**			
Boat Ownership:***			
Certifier's Signature:			
Certifier's Name (Print):			
Certifier's Position:			
Certifier's Street Address:			
Certifier's City/State/Zip:			
Certifier's Phone Number:			

Legend: *Sailing Done: [D] Daysailing, [C] Cruising, [R] Racing.

**Position: [S] Skipper, [M] Mate, [N] Navigator, [C] Crew.

***Ownership: [R] Rental Daysailer, [B] Bareboat Cruising, [C] Crewed Cruising,

[F] Friend's Boat, [O] Own Boat.

Notes:

Trip:	58	59	60
Date:			
Location:			
From:			
To:			
Average Miles from Shore:			
Maximum Miles from Shore:			
Boat Name:			
Boat Type & Rig:			
Documentation or Reg. No.:			
Length:			
Gross Tons.			
Engine Horsepower:			
Type of Sailing Done:*			
Position on Boat:**			
Boat Ownership:***			
Certifier's Signature:			
Certifier's Name (Print):			
Certifier's Position:			
Certifier's Street Address:			
Certifier's City/State/Zip:			
Certifier's Phone Number:			

Legend: *Sailing Done: [D] Daysailing, [C] Cruising, [R] Racing.

**Position: [S] Skipper, [M] Mate, [N] Navigator, [C] Crew.

***Ownership: [R] Rental Daysailer, [B] Bareboat Cruising, [C] Crewed Cruising,

[F] Friend's Boat, [O] Own Boat.

Notes:

Trip:	61	62	63
Date:			
Location:			
From:			
To:			
Average Miles from Shore:			
Maximum Miles from Shore:			
Boat Name:			
Boat Type & Rig:			
Documentation or Reg. No.:			
Length:			
Gross Tons:			
Engine Horsepower:			
Type of Sailing Done:*			
Position on Boat:**			
Boat Ownership:***			
Certifier's Signature:			
Certifier's Name (Print):			
Certifier's Position:			
Certifier's Street Address:			
Certifier's City/State/Zip:			
Certifier's Phone Number:			

Legend: *Sailing Done: [D] Daysailing, [C] Cruising, [R] Racing.

**Position: [S] Skipper, [M] Mate, [N] Navigator, [C] Crew.

***Ownership: [R] Rental Daysailer, [B] Bareboat Cruising, [C] Crewed Cruising,

[F] Friend's Boat, [O] Own Boat.

Notes:

Trip:	64	65	66
Date:			
Location:			
From:			
To:			
Average Miles from Shore:			
Maximum Miles from Shore:			
Boat Name:			
Boat Type & Rig:			
Documentation or Reg. No.:			
Length:			
Gross Tons:			
Engine Horsepower:			
Type of Sailing Done:*			
Position on Boat:**			
Boat Ownership:***			
Certifier's Signature:			
Certifier's Name (Print):			
Certifier's Position:			
Certifier's Street Address:			
Certifier's City/State/Zip:			
Certifier's Phone Number:			

Legend: *Sailing Done: [D] Daysailing, [C] Cruising, [R] Racing.

**Position: [S] Skipper, [M] Mate, [N] Navigator, [C] Crew.

***Ownership: [R] Rental Daysailer, [B] Bareboat Cruising, [C] Crewed Cruising,

[F] Friend's Boat, [O] Own Boat.

Notes:

Trip:	67	68	69
Date:			
Location:			
From:			
To:			
Average Miles from Shore:			
Maximum Miles from Shore:			
Boat Name:			
Boat Type & Rig:			
Documentation or Reg. No.:			
Length:			
Gross Tons:			
Engine Horsepower:			
Type of Sailing Done:*			
Position on Boat:**			
Boat Ownership:***			
Certifier's Signature:			
Certifier's Name (Print):			
Certifier's Position:			
Certifier's Street Address:			
Certifier's City/State/Zip:			
Certifier's Phone Number:			

Legend: *Sailing Done: [D] Daysailing, [C] Cruising, [R] Racing.

**Position: [S] Skipper, [M] Mate, [N] Navigator, [C] Crew.

***Ownership: [R] Rental Daysailer, [B] Bareboat Cruising, [C] Crewed Cruising,

[F] Friend's Boat, [O] Own Boat.

Notes:

Trip:	70	71	72
Date:			
Location:			
From:			
To:			
Average Miles from Shore:			
Maximum Miles from Shore:			
Boat Name:			
Boat Type & Rig:			
Documentation or Reg. No.:			
Length:			
Gross Tons:			
Engine Horsepower:			
Type of Sailing Done:*			
Position on Boat:**			
Boat Ownership:***			
Certifier's Signature:			
Certifier's Name (Print):			
Certifier's Position:			
Certifier's Street Address:			
Certifier's City/State/Zip:			
Certifier's Phone Number:			

Legend: *Sailing Done: [D] Daysailing, [C] Cruising, [R] Racing.

**Position: [S] Skipper, [M] Mate, [N] Navigator, [C] Crew.

***Ownership: [R] Rental Daysailer, [B] Bareboat Cruising, [C] Crewed Cruising,

[F] Friend's Boat, [O] Own Boat.

Notes:

Trip:	73	74	75
Date:			
Location:			
From:			
To:			
Average Miles from Shore:			
Maximum Miles from Shore:			
Boat Name:			
Boat Type & Rig:			
Documentation or Reg. No.:			
Length:			
Gross Tons:			
Engine Horsepower:			
Type of Sailing Done:*			
Position on Boat:**			
Boat Ownership:***			
Certifier's Signature:			
Certifier's Name (Print):			
Certifier's Position:			
Certifier's Street Address:			
Certifier's City/State/Zip:			
Certifier's Phone Number:			

Legend: *Sailing Done: [D] Daysailing, [C] Cruising, [R] Racing.

**Position: [S] Skipper, [M] Mate, [N] Navigator, [C] Crew.

***Ownership: [R] Rental Daysailer, [B] Bareboat Cruising, [C] Crewed Cruising,

[F] Friend's Boat, [O] Own Boat.

Notes:

Trip:	76	77	78
Date:			
Location:			
From:			
To:			
Average Miles from Shore:			
Maximum Miles from Shore:			
Boat Name:			
Boat Type & Rig:			
Documentation or Reg. No.:			
Length:			
Gross Tons:			
Engine Horsepower:			
Type of Sailing Done:*			
Position on Boat:**			
Boat Ownership:***			
Certifier's Signature:			
Certifier's Name (Print):			
Certifier's Position:			
Certifier's Street Address:			
Certifier's City/State/Zip:			
Certifier's Phone Number:			

Legend: *Sailing Done: [D] Daysailing, [C] Cruising, [R] Racing.

**Position: [S] Skipper, [M] Mate, [N] Navigator, [C] Crew.

***Ownership: [R] Rental Daysailer, [B] Bareboat Cruising, [C] Crewed Cruising,

[F] Friend's Boat, [O] Own Boat.

Notes:

Trip:	79	80	81
Date:			
Location:			
From:			
To:			
Average Miles from Shore:			
Maximum Miles from Shore:			
Boat Name:			
Boat Type & Rig:			
Documentation or Reg. No.:			
Length:			
Gross Tons:			
Engine Horsepower:			
Type of Sailing Done:*			
Position on Boat:**			
Boat Ownership:***			
Certifier's Signature:			
Certifier's Name (Print):			
Certifier's Position:			
Certifier's Street Address:			
Certifier's City/State/Zip:			
Certifier's Phone Number:			

Legend: *Sailing Done: [D] Daysailing, [C] Cruising, [R] Racing.

**Position: [S] Skipper, [M] Mate, [N] Navigator, [C] Crew.

***Ownership: [R] Rental Daysailer, [B] Bareboat Cruising, [C] Crewed Cruising,

[F] Friend's Boat, [O] Own Boat.

Notes:

Trip:	82	83	84
Date:			
Location:			
From:			
To:			
Average Miles from Shore:			
Maximum Miles from Shore:			
Boat Name:			
Boat Type & Rig:			
Documentation or Reg. No.:			
Length:			
Gross Tons:			
Engine Horsepower:			
Type of Sailing Done:*			
Position on Boat:**			
Boat Ownership:***			
Certifier's Signature:			
Certifier's Name (Print):			
Certifier's Position:			
Certifier's Street Address:			
Certifier's City/State/Zip:			
Certifier's Phone Number:			

Legend: *Sailing Done: [D] Daysailing, [C] Cruising, [R] Racing.

**Position: [S] Skipper, [M] Mate, [N] Navigator, [C] Crew.

***Ownership: [R] Rental Daysailer, [B] Bareboat Cruising, [C] Crewed Cruising,

[F] Friend's Boat, [O] Own Boat.

Notes:

Trip:	85	86	87
Date:			
Location:			
From:			
To:			
Average Miles from Shore:			
Maximum Miles from Shore:			
Boat Name:			
Boat Type & Rig:			
Documentation or Reg. No.:			
Length:			
Gross Tons:			
Engine Horsepower:			
Type of Sailing Done:*			
Position on Boat:**			
Boat Ownership:***			
Certifier's Signature:			
Certifier's Name (Print):			
Certifier's Position:			
Certifier's Street Address:			
Certifier's City/State/Zip:			
Certifier's Phone Number:			

Legend: *Sailing Done: [D] Daysailing, [C] Cruising, [R] Racing.

**Position: [S] Skipper, [M] Mate, [N] Navigator, [C] Crew.

***Ownership: [R] Rental Daysailer, [B] Bareboat Cruising, [C] Crewed Cruising,

[F] Friend's Boat, [O] Own Boat.

Notes:

Trip:	88	89	90
Date:			
Location:			
From:			
To:			
Average Miles from Shore:			
Maximum Miles from Shore:			
Boat Name:			
Boat Type & Rig:			
Documentation or Reg. No.:			
Length:			
Gross Tons:			
Engine Horsepower:			
Type of Sailing Done:*			
Position on Boat:**			
Boat Ownership:***			
Certifier's Signature:			
Certifier's Name (Print):			
Certifier's Position:			
Certifier's Street Address:			
Certifier's City/State/Zip:			
Certifier's Phone Number:			

Legend: *Sailing Done: [D] Daysailing, [C] Cruising, [R] Racing.

**Position: [S] Skipper, [M] Mate, [N] Navigator, [C] Crew.

***Ownership: [R] Rental Daysailer, [B] Bareboat Cruising, [C] Crewed Cruising,

[F] Friend's Boat, [O] Own Boat.

Notes:

Trip:	91	92	93
Date:			
Location:			
From:			
To:			
Average Miles from Shore:			
Maximum Miles from Shore:			
Boat Name:			
Boat Type & Rig:			
Documentation or Reg. No.:			
Length:			
Gross Tons:			
Engine Horsepower:			
Type of Sailing Done:*			
Position on Boat:**			
Boat Ownership:***			
Certifier's Signature:			
Certifier's Name (Print):			
Certifier's Position:			
Certifier's Street Address:			
Certifier's City/State/Zip:			
Certifier's Phone Number:			

Legend: *Sailing Done: [D] Daysailing, [C] Cruising, [R] Racing.

**Position: [S] Skipper, [M] Mate, [N] Navigator, [C] Crew.

***Ownership: [R] Rental Daysailer, [B] Bareboat Cruising, [C] Crewed Cruising,

[F] Friend's Boat, [O] Own Boat.

Notes:

Trip:	94	95	96
Date:			
Location:			
From:			
To:			
Average Miles from Shore:			
Maximum Miles from Shore:			
Boat Name:			
Boat Type & Rig:			
Documentation or Reg. No.:			
Length:			
Gross Tons:			
Engine Horsepower:			
Type of Sailing Done:*			
Position on Boat:**			
Boat Ownership:***			
Certifier's Signature:			
Certifier's Name (Print):			
Certifier's Position:			
Certifier's Street Address:			
Certifier's City/State/Zip:			
Certifier's Phone Number:			

Legend: *Sailing Done: [D] Daysailing, [C] Cruising, [R] Racing.

**Position: [S] Skipper, [M] Mate, [N] Navigator, [C] Crew.

***Ownership: [R] Rental Daysailer, [B] Bareboat Cruising, [C] Crewed Cruising,

[F] Friend's Boat, [O] Own Boat.

Notes:

Trip:	97	98	99
Date:			
Location:			
From:			
To:			
Average Miles from Shore:			
Maximum Miles from Shore:			
Boat Name:			
Boat Type & Rig:			
Documentation or Reg. No.:			
Length:			
Gross Tons:			
Engine Horsepower:			
Type of Sailing Done:*			
Position on Boat:**			
Boat Ownership:***			
Certifier's Signature:			
Certifier's Name (Print):			
Certifier's Position:			
Certifier's Street Address:			
Certifier's City/State/Zip:			
Certifier's Phone Number:			

Legend: *Sailing Done: [D] Daysailing, [C] Cruising, [R] Racing.

**Position: [S] Skipper, [M] Mate, [N] Navigator, [C] Crew.

***Ownership: [R] Rental Daysailer, [B] Bareboat Cruising, [C] Crewed Cruising,

[F] Friend's Boat, [O] Own Boat.

Notes:

Trip:	100	101	102
Date:			
Location:			
From:			
To:			
Average Miles from Shore:			
Maximum Miles from Shore:			
Boat Name:			
Boat Type & Rig:			
Documentation or Reg. No.:			
Length:			
Gross Tons:			
Engine Horsepower:			
Type of Sailing Done:*			
Position on Boat:**			
Boat Ownership:***			
Certifier's Signature:			
Certifier's Name (Print):			
Certifier's Position:			
Certifier's Street Address:			
Certifier's City/State/Zip:			
Certifier's Phone Number:			

Legend: *Sailing Done: [D] Daysailing, [C] Cruising, [R] Racing.

**Position: [S] Skipper, [M] Mate, [N] Navigator, [C] Crew.

***Ownership: [R] Rental Daysailer, [B] Bareboat Cruising, [C] Crewed Cruising,

[F] Friend's Boat, [O] Own Boat.

Notes:

Trip:	103	104	105
Date:			
Location:			
From:			
To:			
Average Miles from Shore:			
Maximum Miles from Shore:			
Boat Name:			
Boat Type & Rig:			
Documentation or Reg. No.:			
Length:			
Gross Tons:			
Engine Horsepower:			
Type of Sailing Done:*			
Position on Boat:**			
Boat Ownership:***			
Certifier's Signature:			
Certifier's Name (Print):			
Certifier's Position:			
Certifier's Street Address:			
Certifier's City/State/Zip:			
Certifier's Phone Number:			

Legend: *Sailing Done: [D] Daysailing, [C] Cruising, [R] Racing.

**Position: [S] Skipper, [M] Mate, [N] Navigator, [C] Crew.

***Ownership: [R] Rental Daysailer, [B] Bareboat Cruising, [C] Crewed Cruising,

[F] Friend's Boat, [O] Own Boat.

Notes:

Trip:	106	107	108
Date:			
Location:			
From:			
To:			
Average Miles from Shore:			
Maximum Miles from Shore:			
Boat Name:			
Boat Type & Rig:			
Documentation or Reg. No.:			
Length:			
Gross Tons:			
Engine Horsepower:			
Type of Sailing Done:*			
Position on Boat:**			
Boat Ownership:***			
Certifier's Signature:			
Certifier's Name (Print):			
Certifier's Position:			
Certifier's Street Address:			
Certifier's City/State/Zip:			
Certifier's Phone Number:			

Legend: *Sailing Done: [D] Daysailing, [C] Cruising, [R] Racing.

**Position: [S] Skipper, [M] Mate, [N] Navigator, [C] Crew.

***Ownership: [R] Rental Daysailer, [B] Bareboat Cruising, [C] Crewed Cruising,

[F] Friend's Boat, [O] Own Boat.

Notes:

Trip:	109	110	111
Date:			
Location:			
From:			
To:			
Average Miles from Shore:			
Maximum Miles from Shore:			
Boat Name:			
Boat Type & Rig:			
Documentation or Reg. No.:			
Length:			
Gross Tons:			
Engine Horsepower:			
Type of Sailing Done:*			
Position on Boat:**			
Boat Ownership:***			
Certifier's Signature:			
Certifier's Name (Print):			
Certifier's Position:			
Certifier's Street Address:			
Certifier's City/State/Zip:			
Certifier's Phone Number:			

Legend: *Sailing Done: [D] Daysailing, [C] Cruising, [R] Racing.

**Position: [S] Skipper, [M] Mate, [N] Navigator, [C] Crew.

***Ownership: [R] Rental Daysailer, [B] Bareboat Cruising, [C] Crewed Cruising,

[F] Friend's Boat, [O] Own Boat.

Notes:

Trip:	112	113	114
Date:			
Location:			
From:			
To:			
Average Miles from Shore:			
Maximum Miles from Shore:			
Boat Name:			
Boat Type & Rig:			
Documentation or Reg. No.:			
Length:			
Gross Tons:			
Engine Horsepower:			
Type of Sailing Done.*			
Position on Boat:**			
Boat Ownership:***			
Certifier's Signature:			
Certifier's Name (Print):			
Certifier's Position:			
Certifier's Street Address:			
Certifier's City/State/Zip:			
Certifier's Phone Number:			

Legend: *Sailing Done: [D] Daysailing, [C] Cruising, [R] Racing.

**Position: [S] Skipper, [M] Mate, [N] Navigator, [C] Crew.

***Ownership: [R] Rental Daysailer, [B] Bareboat Cruising, [C] Crewed Cruising,

[F] Friend's Boat, [O] Own Boat.

Notes:

Trip:	115	116	117
Date:			
Location:			
From:			
To:			
Average Miles from Shore:			
Maximum Miles from Shore:			
Boat Name:			
Boat Type & Rig:			
Documentation or Reg. No.:			
Length:			
Gross Tons:			
Engine Horsepower:			
Type of Sailing Done:*			
Position on Boat:**			
Boat Ownership:***			
Certifier's Signature:			
Certifier's Name (Print):			
Certifier's Position:			
Certifier's Street Address:			
Certifier's City/State/Zip:			
Certifier's Phone Number:			

Legend: *Sailing Done: [D] Daysailing, [C] Cruising, [R] Racing.

**Position: [S] Skipper, [M] Mate, [N] Navigator, [C] Crew.

***Ownership: [R] Rental Daysailer, [B] Bareboat Cruising, [C] Crewed Cruising,

[F] Friend's Boat, [O] Own Boat.

Notes:

Trip:	118	119	120
Date:			
Location:			
From:			
To:			
Average Miles from Shore:			
Maximum Miles from Shore:			
Boat Name:			
Boat Type & Rig:			
Documentation or Reg. No.:			
Length:			
Gross Tons:			
Engine Horsepower:			
Type of Sailing Done:*			
Position on Boat:**			
Boat Ownership:***			
Certifier's Signature:			
Certifier's Name (Print):			
Certifier's Position:			
Certifier's Street Address:			
Certifier's City/State/Zip:			
Certifier's Phone Number:			

Legend: *Sailing Done: [D] Daysailing, [C] Cruising, [R] Racing.

**Position: [S] Skipper, [M] Mate, [N] Navigator, [C] Crew.

***Ownership: [R] Rental Daysailer, [B] Bareboat Cruising, [C] Crewed Cruising,

[F] Friend's Boat, [O] Own Boat.

Notes:

Trip:	121	122	123
Date:			
Location:			
From:			
To:			
Average Miles from Shore:			
Maximum Miles from Shore:			
Boat Name:			
Boat Type & Rig:			
Documentation or Reg. No.:			
Length:			
Gross Tons:			
Engine Horsepower:			
Type of Sailing Done:*			
Position on Boat:**			
Boat Ownership:***			
Certifier's Signature:			
Certifier's Name (Print):			
Certifier's Position:			
Certifier's Street Address:			
Certifier's City/State/Zip:			
Certifier's Phone Number:			

Legend: *Sailing Done: [D] Daysailing, [C] Cruising, [R] Racing.

**Position: [S] Skipper, [M] Mate, [N] Navigator, [C] Crew.

***Ownership: [R] Rental Daysailer, [B] Bareboat Cruising, [C] Crewed Cruising,

[F] Friend's Boat, [O] Own Boat.

Notes:

Trip:	124	125	126
Date:			
Location:			
From:			
To:			
Average Miles from Shore:			
Maximum Miles from Shore:			
Boat Name:			
Boat Type & Rig:			
Documentation or Reg. No.:			
Length:			
Gross Tons:			
Engine Horsepower:			
Type of Sailing Done:*			
Position on Boat:**			
Boat Ownership:***			
Certifier's Signature:			
Certifier's Name (Print):			
Certifier's Position:			
Certifier's Street Address:			
Certifier's City/State/Zip:			
Certifier's Phone Number:			

Legend: *Sailing Done: [D] Daysailing, [C] Cruising, [R] Racing.

**Position: [S] Skipper, [M] Mate, [N] Navigator, [C] Crew.

***Ownership: [R] Rental Daysailer, [B] Bareboat Cruising, [C] Crewed Cruising,

[F] Friend's Boat, [O] Own Boat.

Notes:

Trip:	127	128	129
Date:			
Location:			
From:			
To:			
Average Miles from Shore:			
Maximum Miles from Shore:			
Boat Name:			
Boat Type & Rig:			
Documentation or Reg. No.:			
Length:			
Gross Tons:			
Engine Horsepower:			
Type of Sailing Done:*			
Position on Boat:**			
Boat Ownership:***			
Certifier's Signature:			
Certifier's Name (Print):			
Certifier's Position:			
Certifier's Street Address:			
Certifier's City/State/Zip:			
Certifier's Phone Number:			

Legend: *Sailing Done: [D] Daysailing, [C] Cruising, [R] Racing.

**Position: [S] Skipper, [M] Mate, [N] Navigator, [C] Crew.

***Ownership: [R] Rental Daysailer, [B] Bareboat Cruising, [C] Crewed Cruising,

[F] Friend's Boat, [O] Own Boat.

Notes:

Trip:	130	131	132
Date:			
Location:			
From:			
To:			
Average Miles from Shore:			
Maximum Miles from Shore:			
Boat Name:			
Boat Type & Rig:			
Documentation or Reg. No.:			
Length:			
Gross Tons:			
Engine Horsepower:			
Type of Sailing Done:*			
Position on Boat:**			
Boat Ownership:***			
Certifier's Signature:			
Certifier's Name (Print):			
Certifier's Position:			
Certifier's Street Address:			
Certifier's City/State/Zip:			
Certifier's Phone Number:			

Legend: *Sailing Done: [D] Daysailing, [C] Cruising, [R] Racing.

**Position: [S] Skipper, [M] Mate, [N] Navigator, [C] Crew.

***Ownership: [R] Rental Daysailer, [B] Bareboat Cruising, [C] Crewed Cruising,

[F] Friend's Boat, [O] Own Boat.

Notes:

Trip:	133	134	135
Date:			
Location:			
From:			
To:			
Average Miles from Shore:			
Maximum Miles from Shore:			
Boat Name:			
Boat Type & Rig:			
Documentation or Reg. No.:			
Length:			
Gross Tons:			
Engine Horsepower:			
Type of Sailing Done:*			
Position on Boat:**			
Boat Ownership:***			
Certifier's Signature:			
Certifier's Name (Print):			
Certifier's Position:			
Certifier's Street Address:			
Certifier's City/State/Zip:			
Certifier's Phone Number:			

Legend: *Sailing Done: [D] Daysailing, [C] Cruising, [R] Racing.

**Position: [S] Skipper, [M] Mate, [N] Navigator, [C] Crew.

***Ownership: [R] Rental Daysailer, [B] Bareboat Cruising, [C] Crewed Cruising,

[F] Friend's Boat, [O] Own Boat.

Notes:

Trip:	136	137	138
Date:			
Location:			
From:			
To:			
Average Miles from Shore:			
Maximum Miles from Shore:			
Boat Name:			
Boat Type & Rig:			
Documentation or Reg. No.:			
Length:			
Gross Tons:			
Engine Horsepower:			
Type of Sailing Done:*			
Position on Boat:**			
Boat Ownership:***			
Certifier's Signature:			
Certifier's Name (Print):			
Certifier's Position:			
Certifier's Street Address:			
Certifier's City/State/Zip:			
Certifier's Phone Number:			

Legend: *Sailing Done: [D] Daysailing, [C] Cruising, [R] Racing.

**Position: [S] Skipper, [M] Mate, [N] Navigator, [C] Crew.

***Ownership: [R] Rental Daysailer, [B] Bareboat Cruising, [C] Crewed Cruising,

[F] Friend's Boat, [O] Own Boat.

Notes:

Trip:	139	140	141
Date:			
Location:			
From:			
To:			
Average Miles from Shore:			
Maximum Miles from Shore:			
Boat Name:			
Boat Type & Rig:			
Documentation or Reg. No.:			
Length:			
Gross Tons:			
Engine Horsepower:			
Type of Sailing Done:*			
Position on Boat:**			
Boat Ownership:***			
Certifier's Signature:			
Certifier's Name (Print):			
Certifier's Position:			
Certifier's Street Address:			
Certifier's City/State/Zip:			
Certifier's Phone Number:			

Legend: *Sailing Done: [D] Daysailing, [C] Cruising, [R] Racing.

**Position: [S] Skipper, [M] Mate, [N] Navigator, [C] Crew.

***Ownership: [R] Rental Daysailer, [B] Bareboat Cruising, [C] Crewed Cruising,

[F] Friend's Boat, [O] Own Boat.

Notes:

Trip:	142	143	144
Date:			
Location:			
From:			
To:			
Average Miles from Shore:			
Maximum Miles from Shore:			
Boat Name:			
Boat Type & Rig:			
Documentation or Reg. No.:			
Length:			
Gross Tons:			
Engine Horsepower:			
Type of Sailing Done:*			
Position on Boat:**			
Boat Ownership:***			
Certifier's Signature:			
Certifier's Name (Print):			
Certifier's Position:			
Certifier's Street Address:			
Certifier's City/State/Zip:			
Certifier's Phone Number:			

Legend: *Sailing Done: [D] Daysailing, [C] Cruising, [R] Racing.

**Position: [S] Skipper, [M] Mate, [N] Navigator, [C] Crew.

***Ownership: [R] Rental Daysailer, [B] Bareboat Cruising, [C] Crewed Cruising,

[F] Friend's Boat, [O] Own Boat.

Notes:

Trip:	145	146	147
Date:			
Location:			
From:			
To:			
Average Miles from Shore:			
Maximum Miles from Shore:			
Boat Name:			
Boat Type & Rig:			
Documentation or Reg. No.:			
Length:			
Gross Tons:			
Engine Horsepower:			
Type of Sailing Done:*			
Position on Boat:**			
Boat Ownership:***			
Certifier's Signature:			
Certifier's Name (Print):			
Certifier's Position:			
Certifier's Street Address:			
Certifier's City/State/Zip:			
Certifier's Phone Number:			

Legend: *Sailing Done: [D] Daysailing, [C] Cruising, [R] Racing.

**Position: [S] Skipper, [M] Mate, [N] Navigator, [C] Crew.

***Ownership: [R] Rental Daysailer, [B] Bareboat Cruising, [C] Crewed Cruising,

[F] Friend's Boat, [O] Own Boat.

Notes:

Trip:	148	149	150
Date:			
Location:			
From:			
To:			
Average Miles from Shore:			
Maximum Miles from Shore:			
Boat Name:			
Boat Type & Rig:			
Documentation or Reg. No.:			
Length:			
Gross Tons:			
Engine Horsepower:			
Type of Sailing Done:*			
Position on Boat:**			
Boat Ownership:***			
Certifier's Signature:			
Certifier's Name (Print):			
Certifier's Position:			
Certifier's Street Address:			
Certifier's City/State/Zip:			
Certifier's Phone Number:			

Legend: *Sailing Done: [D] Daysailing, [C] Cruising, [R] Racing.

**Position: [S] Skipper, [M] Mate, [N] Navigator, [C] Crew.

***Ownership: [R] Rental Daysailer, [B] Bareboat Cruising, [C] Crewed Cruising,

[F] Friend's Boat, [O] Own Boat.

Notes:

Trip:	151	152	153
Date:			
Location:			
From:			
To:			
Average Miles from Shore:			
Maximum Miles from Shore:			
Boat Name:			
Boat Type & Rig:			
Documentation or Reg. No.:			
Length:			
Gross Tons:			
Engine Horsepower:			
Type of Sailing Done:*			
Position on Boat:**			
Boat Ownership:***			
Certifier's Signature:			
Certifier's Name (Print):			
Certifier's Position:			
Certifier's Street Address:			
Certifier's City/State/Zip:			
Certifier's Phone Number:			

Legend: *Sailing Done: [D] Daysailing, [C] Cruising, [R] Racing.

**Position: [S] Skipper, [M] Mate, [N] Navigator, [C] Crew.

***Ownership: [R] Rental Daysailer, [B] Bareboat Cruising, [C] Crewed Cruising,

[F] Friend's Boat, [O] Own Boat.

Notes:

Trip:	154	155	156
Date:			
Location:			
From:			
To:			
Average Miles from Shore:			
Maximum Miles from Shore:			
Boat Name:			
Boat Type & Rig:			
Documentation or Reg. No.:			
Length:			
Gross Tons:			
Engine Horsepower:			
Type of Sailing Done:*			
Position on Boat:**			
Boat Ownership:***			
Certifier's Signature:			
Certifier's Name (Print):			
Certifier's Position:			
Certifier's Street Address:			
Certifier's City/State/Zip:			
Certifier's Phone Number:			

Legend: *Sailing Done: [D] Daysailing, [C] Cruising, [R] Racing.

**Position: [S] Skipper, [M] Mate, [N] Navigator, [C] Crew.

***Ownership: [R] Rental Daysailer, [B] Bareboat Cruising, [C] Crewed Cruising,

[F] Friend's Boat, [O] Own Boat.

Notes:

Trip:	157	158	159
Date:			
Location:			
From:			
To:			
Average Miles from Shore:			
Maximum Miles from Shore:			
Boat Name:			
Boat Type & Rig:			
Documentation or Reg. No.:			
Length:			
Gross Tons:			
Engine Horsepower:			
Type of Sailing Done:*			
Position on Boat:**			
Boat Ownership:***			
Certifier's Signature:			
Certifier's Name (Print):			
Certifier's Position:			
Certifier's Street Address:			
Certifier's City/State/Zip:			
Certifier's Phone Number:			

Legend: *Sailing Done: [D] Daysailing, [C] Cruising, [R] Racing.

**Position: [S] Skipper, [M] Mate, [N] Navigator, [C] Crew.

***Ownership: [R] Rental Daysailer, [B] Bareboat Cruising, [C] Crewed Cruising,

[F] Friend's Boat, [O] Own Boat.

Notes:

Trip:	160	161	162
Date:			
Location:			
From:			
To:			
Average Miles from Shore:			
Maximum Miles from Shore:			
Boat Name:			
Boat Type & Rig:			
Documentation or Reg. No.:			
Length:			
Gross Tons:			
Engine Horsepower:			
Type of Sailing Done:*			
Position on Boat:**			
Boat Ownership:***			
Certifier's Signature:			
Certifier's Name (Print):			
Certifier's Position:			
Certifier's Street Address:			
Certifier's City/State/Zip:			
Certifier's Phone Number:			

Legend: *Sailing Done: [D] Daysailing, [C] Cruising, [R] Racing.

**Position: [S] Skipper, [M] Mate, [N] Navigator, [C] Crew.

***Ownership: [R] Rental Daysailer, [B] Bareboat Cruising, [C] Crewed Cruising,

[F] Friend's Boat, [O] Own Boat.

Notes:

Trip:	163	164	165
Date:			
Location:			
From:			
To:			
Average Miles from Shore:			
Maximum Miles from Shore:			
Boat Name:			
Boat Type & Rig:			
Documentation or Reg. No.:			
Length:			
Gross Tons:			
Engine Horsepower:			
Type of Sailing Done:*			
Position on Boat:**			
Boat Ownership:***			
Certifier's Signature:			
Certifier's Name (Print):			
Certifier's Position:			
Certifier's Street Address:			
Certifier's City/State/Zip:			
Certifier's Phone Number:			

Legend: *Sailing Done: [D] Daysailing, [C] Cruising, [R] Racing.

**Position: [S] Skipper, [M] Mate, [N] Navigator, [C] Crew.

***Ownership: [R] Rental Daysailer, [B] Bareboat Cruising, [C] Crewed Cruising,

[F] Friend's Boat, [O] Own Boat.

Notes:

Trip:	166	167	168
Date:			
Location:			
From:			
To:			
Average Miles from Shore:			
Maximum Miles from Shore:			
Boat Name:			
Boat Type & Rig:			
Documentation or Reg. No.:			
Length:			
Gross Tons:			
Engine Horsepower:			
Type of Sailing Done:*			
Position on Boat:**			
Boat Ownership:***			
Certifier's Signature:			
Certifier's Name (Print):			
Certifier's Position:			
Certifier's Street Address:			
Certifier's City/State/Zip:			
Certifier's Phone Number:			

Legend: *Sailing Done: [D] Daysailing, [C] Cruising, [R] Racing.

**Position: [S] Skipper, [M] Mate, [N] Navigator, [C] Crew.

***Ownership: [R] Rental Daysailer, [B] Bareboat Cruising, [C] Crewed Cruising,

[F] Friend's Boat, [O] Own Boat.

Notes:

Trip:	169	170	171
Date:			
Location:			
From:			
To:			
Average Miles from Shore:			
Maximum Miles from Shore:			
Boat Name:			
Boat Type & Rig:			
Documentation or Reg. No.:			
Length:			
Gross Tons:			
Engine Horsepower:			
Type of Sailing Done:*			
Position on Boat:**			
Boat Ownership:***			
Certifier's Signature:			
Certifier's Name (Print):			
Certifier's Position:			
Certifier's Street Address:			
Certifier's City/State/Zip:			
Certifier's Phone Number:			

Legend: *Sailing Done: [D] Daysailing, [C] Cruising, [R] Racing.

**Position: [S] Skipper, [M] Mate, [N] Navigator, [C] Crew.

***Ownership: [R] Rental Daysailer, [B] Bareboat Cruising, [C] Crewed Cruising,

[F] Friend's Boat, [O] Own Boat.

Notes:

Section Three:
Sailing Tests

This section may be used in two ways: [1] you may test your level of sailing comprehension by checking off those items you feel 100% confident and able to describe or demonstrate. Or, [2] you may take this section to a sailing school, (or the one where you completed your course), and for a fee, have an instructor there grade you on each subject. In this case, the instructor must place his or her initials on the line after each term or category where you were 100% correct. Areas where you need further training should be marked in pencil, so you can study or practice, and return to be retested by the same or a different certifier.

If you wish to "be certified" please have the certifying instructor completely fill out one of the sections below:

Date of Certification:	Date of Certification:
Certifier's Name (Print):	Certifier's Name (Print):
Certifier's Signature: Initials:	Certifier's Signature: Initials:
Address:	Address:
City/State/Zip:	City/State/Zip:
Home Phone: Business Phone:	Home Phone: Business Phone:
School or Other Affiliation:	School or Other Affiliation:
Address:	Address:
City/State/Zip:	City/State/Zip:
Phone:	Phone:
Certifier's Qualifications:	Certifier's Qualifications:

Date of Certification:

Certifier's Name (Print):

Certifier's Signature: Initials:

Address:

City/State/Zip:

Home Phone: Business Phone:

School or Other Affiliation:

Address:

City/State/Zip:

Phone:

Certifier's Qualifications:

Date of Certification:

Certifier's Name (Print):

Certifier's Signature: Initials:

Address:

City/State/Zip:

Home Phone: Business Phone:

School or Other Affiliation:

Address:

City/State/Zip:

Phone:

Certifier's Qualifications:

Date of Certification:

Certifier's Name (Print):

Certifier's Signature: Initials:

Address:

City/State/Zip:

Home Phone: Business Phone:

School or Other Affiliation:

Address:

City/State/Zip:

Phone:

Certifier's Qualifications:

Date of Certification:

Certifier's Name (Print):

Certifier's Signature: Initials:

Address:

City/State/Zip:

Home Phone: Business Phone:

School or Other Affiliation:

Address:

City/State/Zip:

Phone:

Certifier's Qualifications:

Date of Certification:

Certifier's Name (Print):

Certifier's Signature: Initials:

Address:

City/State/Zip:

Home Phone: Business Phone:

School or Other Affiliation:

Address:

City/State/Zip:

Phone:

Certifier's Qualifications:

Date of Certification:

Certifier's Name (Print):

Certifier's Signature: Initials:

Address:

City/State/Zip:

Home Phone: Business Phone:

School or Other Affiliation:

Address:

City/State/Zip:

Phone:

Certifier's Qualifications:

Date of Certification:

Certifier's Name (Print):

Certifier's Signature: Initials:

Address:

City/State/Zip:

Home Phone: Business Phone:

School or Other Affiliation:

Address:

City/State/Zip:

Phone:

Certifier's Qualifications:

Date of Certification:

Certifier's Name (Print):

Certifier's Signature: Initials:

Address:

City/State/Zip:

Home Phone: Business Phone:

School or Other Affiliation:

Address:

City/State/Zip:

Phone:

Certifier's Qualifications:

Date of Certification: Date of Certification:

Certifier's Name (Print):   Certifier's Name (Print):

Certifier's Signature: Initials: Certifier's Signature: Initials:

Address: Address:

City/State/Zip: City/State/Zip:

Home Phone: Business Phone: Home Phone: Business Phone:

School or Other Affiliation: School or Other Affiliation:

Address: Address:

City/State/Zip: City/State/Zip:

Phone: Phone:

Certifier's Qualifications: Certifier's Qualifications:

Date of Certification: Date of Certification:

Certifier's Name (Print):   Certifier's Name (Print):

Certifier's Signature: Initials: Certifier's Signature: Initials:

Address: Address:

City/State/Zip: City/State/Zip:

Home Phone: Business Phone: Home Phone: Business Phone:

School or Other Affiliation: School or Other Affiliation:

Address: Address:

City/State/Zip: City/State/Zip:

Phone: Phone:

Certifier's Qualifications: Certifier's Qualifications:

Basic Sailing

Individual: Check off areas of complete competence. **Certifier:** Initial each correct item.

SAILING TERMS: PARTS OF BOAT

Port & starboard:	Daggerboard:	Downhaul:
Forward:	Upper & lower shrouds:	Boom vang:
Aft:	Spreaders:	Cunningham:
LOA.	Backstay:	Running rigging:
LWL:	Jibstay:	Tiller:
Draft:	Headstay:	Rudder:
Beam:	Tangs:	Halyards:
Foredeck:	Cam cleat:	Sheets:
Bow:	Jam cleat:	Shackles:
Stern:	Gooseneck:	Telltales:
Topsides:	Cockpit:	Winches:
Keel:	Turnbuckles:	Sloop:
Centerboard:	Blocks:	Yawl:
Transom:	Chainplates:	Ketch:
Mast:	Fairleads:	Cutter:
Boom:	Outhaul:	Schooner:

SAILING TERMS: PARTS & TYPES OF SAILS

Head:	Battens:	Draft:
Tack:	Roach:	Sail hanks:
Clew:	Headboard:	Sail slides:
Luff:	Reef cringle:	Mainsail:
Foot:	Tabling:	Jib:
Leech:	Leech cord:	Spinnaker:

SAILING TERMS: TERMS USED UNDERWAY

Wind, veering:	Run:	In irons:
Wind, backing:	Tacking:	Abeam:
Wind, a header:	Jibing:	Astern:
Wind, a lift:	Commands, tacking:	Windward:
Port tack:	Commands, jibing:	Leeward:
Starboard tack:	By the lee:	Leeway:
Closehauled:	Backing the jib, mainsail:	Falling off:
Reach:	Luffing:	Hardening up:
Close reach:	Beating:	Bearing away:
Broad reach:	Steer sailing backwards:	

KNOTS: CAN TIE

Square knot:	Figure eight:
Bowline:	Stopknot:

ON-WATER PROFICIENCY: CAN DEMONSTRATE ABILITY TO

Properly prepare the sails for sailing:	Figure 8's around reaching buoys:
Properly hoist sails, cleat and coil lines:	Figure 8's around windward & leeward buoys:
Steer the boat on a reach:	Set sails properly for all points of sailing:
Steer the boat on a run:	Use jib telltales properly:
Steer the boat closehauled:	Get out of irons:
Give proper commands for tacking:	Find the wind direction:
Give proper commands for jibing:	Pick up a mooring buoy:
Tack the boat:	Properly fold the sails:
Jibe the boat:	

ON-WATER PROFICIENCY: BOATS TESTED IN

Class of Boat:			
Type of Boat:			
Size:			
Rig:			
Date:			

Intermediate Sailing

Individual: Check off areas of complete competence. **Certifier:** Initial each correct item.

SAILING TERMS: GENERAL

Slot effect:	Postive stability:	Planing:
Backwind:	Weather helm, causes:	Spring lines:
Apparent wind:	Lee helm, causes:	Breast line:
Sailing wing & wing:	Balance:	Scope:
Sculling:	Use of a traveler:	Plow anchor:
To turn turtle:	Hull speed:	Danforth anchor:
Center of buoyancy:	Surfing:	Chafe gear:
Broaching:	Center of Lateral Resistance:	

SAILING TERMS: RIGHT OF WAY TERMS & RULES

Stand-on vessel:	Same tack rule:	Overtaking rule:
Give-way vessel:	Opposite tack rule:	

SAILING TERMS: NAVIGATION

Variation:	True course or bearing:	Dividers:
Deviation:	Magnetic course or bearing:	Parallel rules:
Magnetic compass rose:	Degree's distance:	Plotting a course:
Meridians & Parallels:	Minute's distance:	Nuns & Cans:

KNOTS: CAN TIE

Two half hitches:	Eye splice:	Clove hitch:

ON-WATER PROFICIENCY: CAN DEMONSTRATE GENERAL ABILITY

Pick up person overboard:	Set, jibe and douse a spinnaker:
Determine jib lead placement:	Sail backwards:
Sail wing and wing:	Anchor under sail:
Properly set anchor with sufficient scope:	

ON-WATER PROFICIENCY: ABILITY TO SAIL WITHOUT A RUDDER

Sail to a destination without touching the tiller (steering by sails alone):

Head up and fall off: Tack and jibe (in light air):

ON-WATER PROFICIENCY: BOATS TESTED IN

Class of Boat:			
Type of Boat:			
Size:			
Rig:			
Date:			

Notes:

Advanced Sailing

Individual: Check off areas of complete competence. **Certifier:** Initial each correct item.

GENERAL: KNOWLEDGE OF

Draft:	Fill:	Luff round:
Chord:	Turning sail "Inside Out:"	Twist:
Weft and warp:	Broadseaming:	

SAIL SHAPE: KNOWLEDGE OF EFFECT ON SAIL SHAPE OF

A tight leech:	No boom vang on reaches:	Jib lead too far forward:
Excessive mast bend:	Outhaul too loose:	Jib sheet too loose:
Cocked battens:	Cunningham too tight:	Sail shape for bumpy seas:
Traveler to windward:	Mainsheet too tight:	Sail shape for flat water:

JIB LEADS: CAN DESCRIBE

Mast rake's effect on jib lead:	Jib downhaul's effect on jib lead:
Jib halyard's effect on jib lead:	Jib sheet ease effect on jib lead:

EMERGENCIES: REACTS PROPERLY TO THE FOLLOWING

Windward upper shroud breaks:	Mast goes over, lee shore nearby:
Jibstay breaks:	A squall hits, lower which sail?:
Backstay breaks:	List five distress signals:
Windward spreader breaks:	

NAVIGATION: KNOWLEDGE OF

How to apply compass errors to headings:	LOP's:
Origin and/or definition of "Knot:"	A fix and a running fix:
Dead reckoning position:	A range:
Deviation problems:	Tidal current tables:
Variation problems:	Estimated position:
Chart reading problems:	Doubling the angle:

Cruising

Individual: Check off areas of complete competence. **Certifier:** Initial each correct item.

GENERAL: CAN EXPLAIN

Lights on a tug with a tow less than 200 meters astern:

Lights on a tug with a tow 200 meters astern:

Lights on a powerboat over 50 meters in length:

Lights on a trawler dragging nets:

Lights of another sailboat:

How to time lights at night:

Proper order and time for making colors:

Airflow around a high pressure area:	Use of a tripline:
Airflow around a low pressure area:	Two or three ways to raise a stuck anchor:
Gradient winds:	Kedging off:
Thermal winds:	Other methods of getting free when aground:
Geographic winds:	Tidal current tables:
Heaving to:	Estimated position:
Use of storm trysail:	Running fix:
Use of double anchors:	Doubling the angle:

ON-WATER PROFICIENCY: CAN DEMONSTRATE ABILITY

Proper precautions fueling:	Proper cleating and coiling:
Fire extinguisher locations:	Proper tacking and jibing:
Life vest locations:	Proper dinghy towing:
Use of springlines to leave dock:	Proper bouncing or sweating halyards:
Precautions and order for setting sails:	Proper head operation:
Proper reefing procedures:	Proper stove operation:
Proper winch handling and tailing:	Proper man overboard procedures:

ON-WATER PROFICIENCY: BOATS TESTED IN

Class of Boat:			
Type of Boat:			
Size:			
Rig:			
Date:			

Notes:

Racing

GENERAL: CAN EXPLAIN

Favored end of starting line:	Why tack in headers:
A dip start:	When to reach a layline:
Luffing before starting rule:	How to round leeward marks:
Barging rules:	What to do after hitting a mark:
Returning to restart rule:	What causes spinnaker oscillation:
Safe leeward position:	How to reduce broaching:
Backwind zone:	How to use ranges in current:
Blanket zone:	Buoy room rights:
Close cover:	Starting and finishing definition:
Loose cover:	Overlap definition:
Luffing after starting rule:	Tacking and jibing definition:

Notes:

Appendices

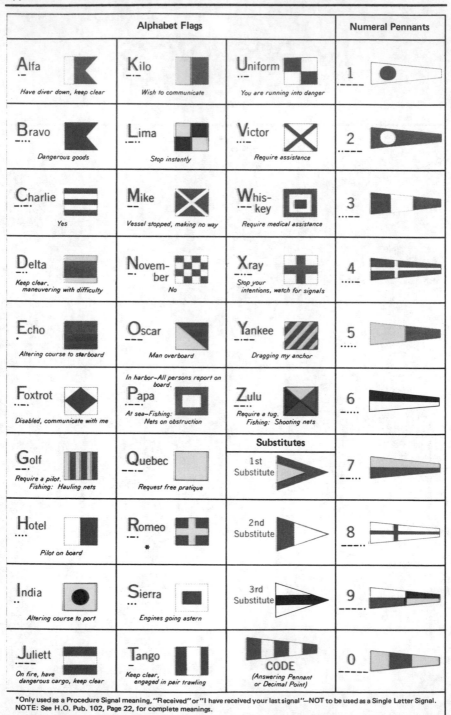

Alphabet Flags			Numeral Pennants

Alfa ▪–
Have diver down, keep clear

Kilo –▪–
Wish to communicate

Uniform ▪▪–
You are running into danger

1 ▪––––

Bravo –▪▪▪
Dangerous goods

Lima ▪–▪▪
Stop instantly

Victor ▪▪▪–
Require assistance

2 ▪▪–––

Charlie –▪–▪
Yes

Mike ––
Vessel stopped, making no way

Whis-key ▪––
Require medical assistance

3 ▪▪▪––

Delta –▪▪
Keep clear, maneuvering with difficulty

Novem-ber –▪
No

Xray –▪▪–
Stop your intentions, watch for signals

4 ▪▪▪▪–

Echo ▪
Altering course to starboard

Oscar –––
Man overboard

Yankee –▪––
Dragging my anchor

5 ▪▪▪▪▪

Foxtrot ▪▪–▪
Disabled, communicate with me

Papa ▪––▪
In harbor–All persons report on board.
At sea–Fishing: Nets on obstruction

Zulu ––▪▪
Require a tug.
Fishing: Shooting nets

6 –▪▪▪▪

Golf ––▪
Require a pilot.
Fishing: Hauling nets

Quebec ––▪–
Request free pratique

Substitutes

1st Substitute

7 ––▪▪▪

Hotel ▪▪▪▪
Pilot on board

Romeo ▪–▪
*

2nd Substitute

8 –––▪▪

India ▪▪
Altering course to port

Sierra ▪▪▪
Engines going astern

3rd Substitute

9 ––––▪

Juliett ▪–––
On fire, have dangerous cargo, keep clear

Tango –
Keep clear, engaged in pair trawling

CODE
(Answering Pennant or Decimal Point)

0 –––––

*Only used as a Procedure Signal meaning, "Received" or "I have received your last signal"—NOT to be used as a Single Letter Signal.
NOTE: See H.O. Pub. 102, Page 22, for complete meanings.

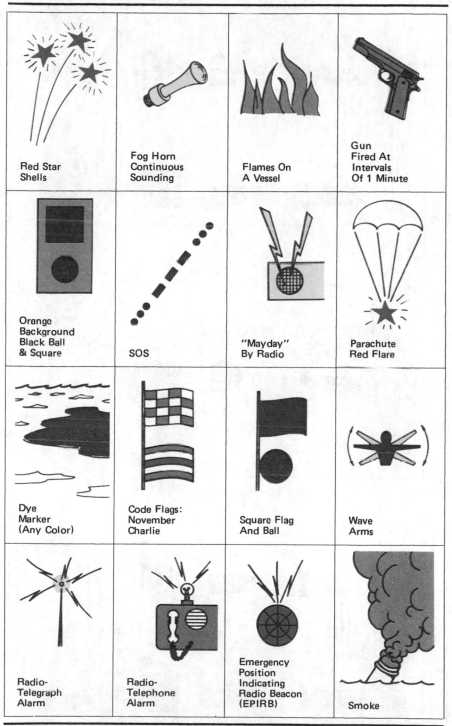

Red Star Shells	Fog Horn Continuous Sounding	Flames On A Vessel	Gun Fired At Intervals Of 1 Minute
Orange Background Black Ball & Square	SOS	"Mayday" By Radio	Parachute Red Flare
Dye Marker (Any Color)	Code Flags: November Charlie	Square Flag And Ball	Wave Arms
Radio-Telegraph Alarm	Radio-Telephone Alarm	Emergency Position Indicating Radio Beacon (EPIRB)	Smoke

Appendix C: Aids to Navigation International/Inland

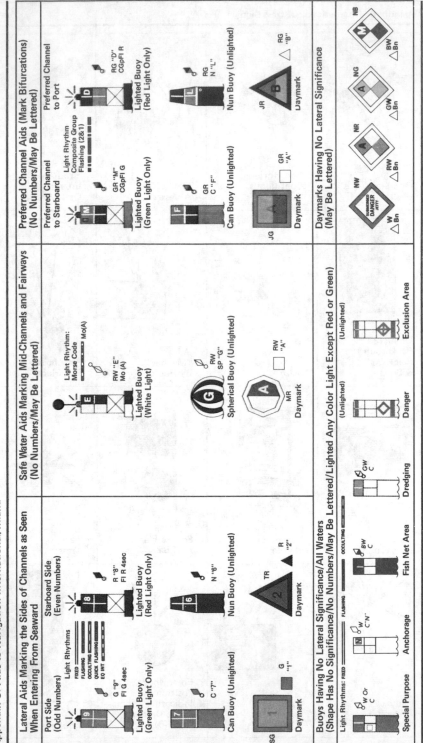

Appendix D: Abbreviations and Symbols Found on Nautical Charts

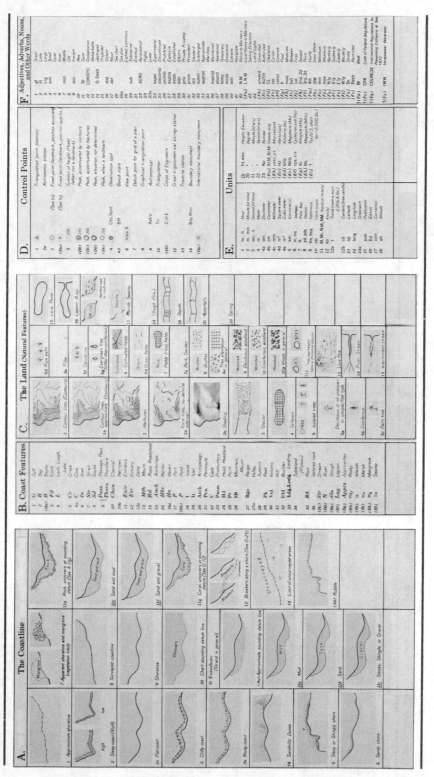

Appendix D: Abbreviations and Symbols Found on Nautical Charts

G. Ports and Harbors

No.	Abbr.	Description
1	Anch	Anchorage (large vessels)
2	Anch	Anchorage (small vessels)
	Hbr	Harbor
	Hrt	Haven
	P	Port
6	Bkw	Breakwater
6a	Dks	Dike
7		Mole
8		Jetty (partly below MHW)
8a		
9		Submerged jetty
	Pier	Pier
10	Spit	Spot
11		Groin (partly below MHW)
11(Ga)	ANCH PROHIB	Anchorage prohibited (screen optional)(See P 25)
12		
12a	QUARANTINE ANCHORAGE	Anchorage reserved
12b		Quarantine anchorage
13	Spoil Area	Spoil ground (See P 11)
13(Ga)	Dumping Ground	Dumping ground (depths may be less than indicated) (Dump Site)
13(G.)	Disposal Area	Disposal areas (Dump Site)
13(Gb)	PROHIBITED DUMPING AREA	Prohibited area (screen optional)
14		Fish stks
14a		Fisheries, Fishing stakes
14b		Fish trap, fish weirs (actual shape charted)
15		Duck blind
15a		Tuna nets (See G 14a)
16	Oys	Oyster bed
17	Ldg, Lndg	Landing place
18		Watering place
19	Whf	Wharf
		Quay

No.	Abbr.	Description
20		Berth
		Anchoring berth
		Berth number
21	Dol	Dolphin
22		Bollard
23		Mooring ring
24		Crane
25		Landing stage
26	Quar	Landing stairs
		Quarantine
27		Lazaret
28	Hbr Mr	Harbor Master
29	Cus Ho	Harbor-master's office
30		Customhouse
31		Fishing harbor
32		Winter harbor
33	B Hbr	Refuge harbor
34		Boat harbor
		Sounding harbor
35		Dock
36		Drydock (actual shape on large-scale charts)
37		Floating dock (actual shape on large-scale charts)
38		Gridiron, Careening grid
39		Patent slip, Slipway, Marine railway
39a	Ramp	Ramp
40		Lock (point upstream)
41		Wetdock
43		Lumber yard
44		Health Office
45		Hulk (actual shape on large-scale charts)
46	PROHIBITED ANCH AREA	Prohibited area (screen optional)
46a		Anchorage for seaplanes
47		Seaplane landing area
49	Under Construction	Work in progress
50		Under construction
		Work projected
1(a)	Subm	Submerged ruins
1(d)	Dump Site	Dump Site

H. Topography (Artificial Features)

No.	Description
1	Road (Rd) or Highway (Hy)
1(Ha)	Highway markers
2	Track, Footpath, or Trail
3	Railway (Ry), (single or double track), Railroad (RR)
3a	Tramway
3b	Railway station
3c	Tunnel (railroad or road)
3d	Embankment, Levee
3f	Cutting
3f	Causeway
4	Overhead power cable (same max feet)
5	Power transmission line
5a	Power transmission mast
6	Prominent telegraph or telephone line
7	Aqueduct, Water pipe
8	Viaduct
8a	Pipeline
9	Vertical beam, power transmitting tower (generally shown intersection plane of reference)
9a	Spring
10	Highway (See H 1)
11	Sewer
12	Culvert
13	Canal, Ditch, Lock, Sluice (point upstream)
14	Bridge (in general)
14a	Stone, concrete bridge (same as H 14)
14b	Wooden bridge (same as H 14)
14c	Iron bridge (same as H 14)
14d	Suspension bridge (same as H 14)
15	Drawbridge (in general)
16	Swing bridge (same as H 15)
16a	Lift bridge
16b	Weighbridge or Bascule bridge
17	Pontoon bridge
17a	Foot-bridge
18	Transporter bridge (same as H 14)
18a	Bridge clearance, vertical
18b	Bridge clearance, horizontal
19	Ferry (Fy)
19(Hb)	Cable ferry
20	Ford
21	Dam
23	Training wall
24	Log boom

I. Buildings and Structures

No.	Abbr.	Symbol	Description
1			City or Town (large scale)
1(a)			City or Town (small scale)
2	Vil		Suburb
3			Village
3a			Buildings in general
4	Cas		Castle
5			House
6			Villa
7			Farm
8			Church
8a	Cath		Cathedral
8b	Spire		Spire, Steeple
9			Roman Catholic Church
10			Temple
11			Chapel
12			Mosque
12a			Minaret
12b			Moslem Shrine
13			Marabout
14	Pag		Pagoda
15			Buddhist Temple, Joss-House
15a			Shinto Shrine
16			Monastery, Convent
17			Calvary, Cross
17a	Cem		Cemetery, Non-Christian
17b			Cemetery, Christian
18			Tank
19			Fort (actual shape charted)
20			Battery
21			Barracks
22			Powder magazine
23			Airplane landing field
24			Airport, large scale (See P 13)
1(d)			Airport, military (small scale)
25			Airport, civil (small scale)
26	St		Street
26a			Avenue
26b			Boulevard
27	Tel		Telegraph
28	Tel Off		Telegraph office
29	PO		Post office
30	Govt Ho		Government house
31			Town hall
32	Hosp		Hospital
33			Slaughterhouse
34	Magz		Magazine
35	MON		Warehouse, Storehouse
36	CUP		Cupola
37	ELEV		Elevator
38	Elev		Elevation, Elevated
39			Shed
40			Zinc roof
41	TR		Ruins
42	ABAND LT HO		Tower
43	WINDMILL		Abandoned lighthouse
43a	WINDMOTOR		Windmill
44	CHIM		Windmotor
45	PIPE		Chimney, Stack
46			Water tower, Standpipe
47	TANK		Oil tank
48			Factory
49			Saw mill
50			Brick kiln
51			Mine, Quarry
52			Well
53	TANK		Cistern
54			Tank
55			Noria
			Fountain

Appendix D: Abbreviations and Symbols Found on Nautical Charts

I. Buildings and Structures (continued)

No.	Abbr.	Description	No.	Abbr.	Description
61	Inst	Institute	72	Sub	Cable
62		Establishment	73		Well
63		Bathing establishment	74		Pyramid
64	Ct Ho	Courthouse	75		Pillar
65	Sch	School	176		Oil derrick
(4a)			(4b)	Ltd	Limited
(4b)	HS	High school	(4b)	Apt	Apartment
66	Univ	University	(4b)	Cap	Capitol
67	Pav	Pavilion	(4b)	Co	Company
68		Hut	(4b)	Corp	Corporation
69		Stadium	(4a)		Landmark (position accurately)(See D 3)
70	T	Telephone	(4b)		Landmark (position approximate)(See Dd)
71		Gas tank, Gasometer			

J. Miscellaneous Stations

No.	Abbr.	Description	No.	Abbr.	Description
1	Sta	Any kind of station	13		Tide signal station
2	Sta	Station	14		Stream signal station
3	CG	Coast Guard station (similar to Lifesaving Station, see J 6)	15		Ice signal station
3 (4a)	WALLIS SANDS	Coast Guard station (when landmark)	16		Time signal station
4	LOOK TR	Lookout station, Watch tower	16a		Manned oceanographic station
5		Lifeboat station	16b		Unmanned oceanographic station
6		Lifesaving station (See J 3)	17		Time ball
7		Rocket station	18		Signal mast
7,8	HL STA	Atas station/Pilots	18a		Mast
9	Sig Sta	Signal station	18b		Flag tower, Flagstaff
10	Sem	Semaphore	19		Flag staff; Signal
11	S Sig Sta	Storm signal station	20	Obs	Observatory
12 (4a)	WEA SIG STA	Nat'l Weather Service signal sta.	21	Off	Office
			22		Bell (on land)
			(4c)	MARINE POLICE	Marine police station
			(4c)	FIREBOAT STATION	Fireboat station

K. Lights

No.	Abbr.	Description	No.	Abbr.	Description
1		Position of light	126	Alt, Al.	Alternating
2	Lt	Light	127	Gp Occ, Gr. Occ.	Group Occulting; Composite group occulting
(4a)		Riprap surrounding light	128	Gp Fl; Gr. Fl.	Group Flashing; Group-Short Flashing
3	Lt Ho	Lighthouse	28a/28b	S-L Fl	Short Long Flashing; Group-Short Flashing
4	AERO	Aeronautical light (See F.22)	29	F Fl	Fixed and Flashing
4a		Marine and air navigation light	30a	F Gp Fl	Fixed and Group Flashing
5		Light beacon	30a	Mo. Al	Morse Code light; two flashes grouped as in letter A)
6		Light vessel; Lightship	31	Rot	Revolving or Rotating light
7		Lantern	42	Per	Period
8		Street lamp	43		Every
9		Reflector	43		With
10		Leading light	44	Vis	Visible (français)
11		Sector light	(4a)	M, Nm, Naut	Nautical mile (See E.4)
12		Directional light	(4b)	m, min	Minutes (See E.4)
14		Harbor light	(4c)	s, sec	Seconds (See E.4)
15		Fishing light	45	Fl	Flash
16		Tidal light	46	Occ	Occultation
17	Priv maint	Private light (maintained by private interests, to be used with caution)	46c	Ecl	Eclipse
21	F	Fixed (steady light)	47	Gp	Group
122	Occ, Oc	Occulting (total duration of light more than dark)	48	Int	Intermittent light
23		Single-Flashing (total duration of light less than dark)	49	SEC	Sector
7 (Rh)	L Fl	Long Flashing (2s or longer)	66	Aux	Auxiliary light
23a	Iso	Isophase (light and dark equal)	51	Var	Varied
124	Qk Fl; Q Qk Fl(Q)	Quick Flashing (60 to one minute, U.S.)	62	Vi	Violet
			61		Purple
25	I Qk Fl(IQ)	Interrupted Quick Flashing	62	Bu	Blue
1 (Rh)	V Qk Fl(VQ)	Continuous Very Quick Flashing	64	G	Green
	VQ (GR)	Group Very Quick	65	Or, Y	Orange
	IVQ	Interrupted Very Quick	66	R	Red
	UQ	International Ultra Quick	67	W	White
25a	S Fl	Short Flashing	67a	Am	Amber
			(4a)	Y	Yellow
			68	OBSC	Obscured
			68a	Fog det Lt	Fog detector light (See N6)

Figures in parentheses are examples

K. Lights (continued)

No.	Abbr.	Description
69		Unwatched light
70	Occas	Occasional light
71	Irreg	Irregular light
72	Prov	Provisional light
73	Temp	Temporary light
(4a)	D Destr	Destroyed
74	Extin	Extinguished light
75		Faint light
76		Upper light
77		Rear light
78		Front light
79		Vertical lights
80	Hor	Horizontal lights
81		Vertical beam
(4a)		Range
(4b)	Exper	Experimental light
74 (4a)		Temporarily replaced by lighted buoy showing the same characteristics
75	TR LB	Temporarily replaced by unlighted buoy
76	TR UB	Temporarily lighted buoy
77	TLB	Temporarily lighted buoy
78	TUB	Temporarily unlighted buoy

L. Buoys and Beacons

No.	Description	No.	Description
1	Approximate position of buoy	127	Bifurcation buoy
2	Light buoy	108	Junction buoy
3	Bell buoy	148	Isolated danger buoy
3a	Gong buoy	140	Wreck buoy
4	Whistle buoy	128a	Obstruction buoy
5	Can or Cylindrical buoy	31	Telegraph-cable buoy
6	Nun or Conical buoy	32	Mooring buoy (colors of mooring buoys never carried)
7	Spherical buoy	32a	Mooring
8	Spar buoy	32b	Mooring buoy with telegraphic communications
9a	Pillar or Spindle buoy	32c	Mooring buoy with telephonic communications
9	Buoy with topmark (ball) (See L 70)	33	Warping buoy
10	Barrel or Ton buoy	34	Quarantine buoy
69	Color unknown	34a	Practice area buoy
(4a)		33	Explosive anchorage buoy
12	Float	44	Aeronautical anchorage buoy
13	Lightship	45	Compass adjustment buoy
14	Outer or Landfall buoy	46	Fish trap (area) buoy
14	Fairway buoy (RWVS)	47	Spoil ground buoy
15	Midchannel buoy (RWVS)	48	Anchorage buoy (marks limits)
16	Starboard-hand buoy (entering from seaward)	49	Private aid to navigation (buoy) (maintained by private interests, use with caution)
17	Port-hand buoy (entering from seaward)		

Appendix D: Abbreviations and Symbols Found on Nautical Charts

L. Buoys and Beacons (continued)

30	Temporary buoy (See K.j, k.l)
30a	Winter buoy
31	Horizontal stripes or bands
32	Vertical stripes
33	Checkered
33a	Diagonal bands
	Dwg
41	W	White
42	B	Black
43	R	Red
44	Y	Yellow
45	G	Green
46	Br	Brown
47	Gy	Gray
48	Bu	Blue
48a	Am	Amber
48b	Or	Orange
51	Floating beacon
52	Fixed beacon (lighted or daybeacon)
52a	Black beacon
	Color unknown
53	Bn	Beacon, in general (See L.52)
54	Tower beacon
55	Cardinal marking system

56	Compass adjustment beacon
57	Topmarks (See L.9)
58	Telegraph-cable (landing) beacon
59	Pile, Piles (See O.30, H.9, 9a)
	Stakes
	Stumps (See O.30)
	Perches
61	CAIRN	Cairn
62	Painted patches
63	TR	Landmark (position accurate) (See D.2)
64	Landmark (position approximate)
	Ref	Reflector
65	MARKER	Range targets, markers
66	Special-purpose buoys
67	Oil installation buoy
	Drilling platform (See Ol, Og)
70	NOTE: Refer to new L-70, on page 11, for aid system used in certain foreign waters
71	RaRef	Radar-reflector (See M.3) (not charted on IALA Sys "A" marks see L.70)
171	LANBY (large auto. nav. buoy)	Superbuoy
172	TANKER terminal buoy (mooring)
173	ODAS (Data buoy)

M. Radio and Radar Stations

1	R Sta	Radio relay-agrk station
2	R T	Radio telephone station
3	R Bn	Radiobeacon
4	R Bn	Circular radiobeacon
5	RD	Directional radiobeacon, Radio range
6		Rotating loop radiobeacon
7	RDF	Radio direction finding station
8		Radio relay mast
8a		Microwave tower
9	R MAST	Radio mast
		Radio tower
9a	TV M	Television mast, Television tower
10	R BN	Radio broadcasting station (commercial)
10a		OTG radio station
11	Ra	Radar station
12	Racon	Radar responder beacon
13	Ra Ref	Radar-reflector (See L.71)
14	Ra (conspic)	Radar conspicuous object
14a		Ramark
15	GFS	Distance finding station (synchronized signals)
16	AERO R Bn	Aeronautical radiobeacon, Radio range
17		Aeronautical radiobeacon
18		Decca station
19	CONSOL Bn	Consol (Consolan) station
19a	AERO R Bn	Aeronautical radio range
19b	Ra Ref Calibration Bn	Radar calibration Beacon
19c	CORINO TR	Loran tower (name)
19d	SPINNING ISLAND	Loran station (name)
19e	R TR	Obstruction light
19f	R Dome	Radar dome
19g		Ultra-high frequency
19h		Very high frequency

N. Fog Signals

1	Fog Sig	Fog-signal station
2		Radio fog-signal station
3		Explosive fog signal
4	GUN	Submarine fog signal
5	SUB-BELL	Submarine fog bell (action of waves)
6	SUB-BELL	Submarine fog bell (mechanical)
7	SUB-OSC	Submarine oscillator
8		Nautophone
9	DIA	Diaphone
10	GUN	Fog gun
11	SIREN	Fog siren
12	HORN	Fog trumpet
13	HORN	Air (Reyphone)
13a	HORN	Electric (Reyphone)
14	BELL	Fog whistle
15	WHIS	Fog whistle
16	HORN	Reed horn
17	GONG	Fog gong
18		Submarine sound signal connected to the shore (See N.5.6,7)
18a		Submarine sound signal not connected to the shore (See N.5.6,7)
19	HORN	Typhon
19a	Fog Det Lt	Fog detector light (See R.68a)
19b		Morse Code fog signal

O. Dangers

11		Wreck showing any portion of hull or superstructure (above sounding datum)
11		Rock which does not cover (height above MHW)
12		Wreck with only masts visible (above sounding datum)
13		Old symbols for wrecks
2		Rock which covers and uncovers with height above chart sounding datum (See foreshore)
3		Rock awash at (near) level of chart sounding datum
3a		Dotted line emphasizes danger to navigation
4		Submerged rock (depth unknown)
4a		Dotted line emphasizes danger to navigation
5		Shoal sounding on isolated rock
6		Submerged rock not dangerous to surface navigation (See O.4)
6a		Oysterts or Ton reps
7		Reef of unknown extent
8		Submarine volcano
9		Discolored water
10		Coral reef, detached (uncovers at sounding datum)
		Coral or Rocky reef, covered at sounding datum (See A.11f, 11g)
14		Sunken wreck dangerous to surface navigation (less than 11 fathoms over wreck) (See A.10, 11g)
15		Wreck over which depth is known
15a		Wreck with depth cleared by wire drag
16		Sunken wreck, not dangerous to surface navigation
17		Foul ground, Foul bottom (fb)
18		Tide rips
19		Eddies
20		Kelp, Seaweed
25		Breakers (See A.12)
26		Submerged rock (See O.4)
27	Obstr	Obstruction
28	Wks	Wreckage
29		Wreckage
29a		Wreck remains (dangerous only for anchoring)
30		Submerged piling (See A.9, 9a, L.59)
		Snags, Submerged stumps
30a		Snags, Submerged stumps
31		Lesser depth possible
32	Unov	Uncov, Dries (See A.10, O.2, 10)
33	Cov	Covers (See O.2, 10)
34	Unov	Uncov (See A.10, O.2, 10)
		Reported (with date)
36		Reported (with name and date)
36	Discol	Discolored (See O.9)
37		Isolated danger
38		Limiting danger line
39		Limit of rocky area
41	PA	Position approximate
42	ED	Existence doubtful
43	PD	Position doubtful
44	Doubtful
45	Reported
46	Unexamined
	LD	Least Depth

Appendix D: Abbreviations and Symbols Found on Nautical Charts

P. Various Limits, etc.

1		Leading line, Range line
2		Transit
3		In line with
4		Limit of sector
15		Channel, Course, Track recommended (marked by buoys or beacons) (see P 23)
15a		Recommended track for deep draft vessels (defined by fixed marks)
15b		Recommended track for deep draft vessels (not defined by fixed marks)
6		Alternate Course
16a		Established traffic separation scheme. One-way traffic lanes (represented by line or zone)
16b		Established traffic separation scheme — Roundabout
16c		Recommended direction of traffic
7		Submarine cable (power telegraph, telephone, etc.)
7a		Submarine cable area
7b		Abandoned submarine cable (includes disused cables)
8		Submarine pipeline
8a		Submarine pipeline area
8b		Abandoned submarine pipeline
3		Maritime limit in general
(PA)		Limit of restricted area
(PA)		Limits of national fishing zones
(Pa)		U.S. Harbor Line
11		Limit of dumping ground, spoil ground (see D 13)
12		Anchorage limit
9		Limit of airport (See I 23, 24)
13a		Limit of military practice areas
14		Limit of sovereignty (Territorial waters)
9		Customs boundary
10		International boundary (also State boundary)
17		Stream limit
18		Fee lines
30		Limit of tide
21		Limit of Navigation
22a		Recommended track not marked by buoys or beacons
22b		Depth is shown where it has been obtained by the cognizant authority
32		District or province limit
33		Reservation line
24		Measured distance
25		Prohibited area (see G 12, 46) (Screen optional)
(PA)		Shipping safety fairway; Two-way traffic
(PA)		Limits of former mine danger area
(PA)		Reference target scale chart
(PA)		Limit of fishing areas (fish trap areas)
(PA)		3-mile Territorial Sea Boundary
		12-mile Contiguous Zone Boundary; headland to headland line
(PA)		COLREGS demarcation line

Q. Soundings

1	SD	Doubtful sounding
2	*85*	No bottom found
3	(12)	Out of position
4		Least depth in narrow channels
5		Dredged channel (with controlling depth indicated)
6		Dredged area
7		Swept channel (See Q 3)
8		Drying (or uncovering) heights above chart sounding datum
9		Swept area, not adequately sounded (shown by purple or green tint)
9a		Swept area adequately sounded (swept by wire drag to depth indicated)
10		Hairline depth figures
10a		Figures for ordinary soundings
11		Soundings taken from foreign charts
12		Soundings taken from older surveys (or smaller scale charts)
13		Echo soundings
14		Sloping figures
15		Upright figures (See Q 10)
16		Bracketed figures (See Q 12)
17		Underlined sounding figures (See L 8)
18		Soundings expressed in fathoms and feet
22		Unsounded area
(Qx)		Stream

R. Depth Contours and Tints

Feet	Fm/Meters		Feet	Fm/Meters
0	0		300	50
6	2		600	100
12	3		1,200	200
18	4		2,400	400
24	5		3,000	500
30	6		6,000	1,000
60	10		12,000	2,000
120	20		18,000	3,000
180	30			
240	40			Or continuous lines, with values

S. Quality of the Bottom

1	Grd	Ground		12	Ck	Chalk	20	Si	Scoriae
2	S	Sand		12a	Ca	Calcareous	21	Ca	Cinders
3	M	Mud, Muddy		13	Qz	Quartz	21a		Ash
4	Oz	Ooze		13a	Sch	Schist	22	Mn	Manganese
5	Ml	Marl		14	Co	Coral	23	Sh	Shells
6	Cy	Clay		14a	Co Hd	Coral head	24	Oys	Oysters
7	G	Gravel		15	Mds	Madrepores	25	Ms	Mussels
8	Sn	Shingle		16	Vol	Volcanic	26	Spg	Sponge
9	P	Pebbles		16a	Vol Ash	Volcanic ash	27	K	Kelp
10	St	Stones		17	La	Lava	28	Wd	Seaweed
11	Rk, rky	Rock, Rocky		18	Pm	Pumice		Sm	Grass
11a	Bld	Boulders		19	T	Tufa	29	Stg	Sea-tangle

S. Quality of the Bottom

31	Spk	Specks		45	stk	Sticky	60	gn	Green
32	Fr	Foraminifera		46	snk		61	yl	Yellow
33	Gl	Globigerina		47	brk	Broken	62	or	Orange
34	Di	Diatoms		47a	grd	Ground (Shells)	63	rd	Red
35	Rd	Radiolaria		48	rt	Rotten	64	br	Brown
36	Pt	Pteropods		49	str	Streaky	65	ch	Chocolate
37	Po	Polyzoa		50	spk	Speckled	66	Gr	Gray
38	Cni	Cirripeda		51	gty	Gritty	67	lt	Light
38a	Fu	Fucus		52	dec	Decayed	68	dk	Dark
38b	Ma	Mattes		53	fly	Flinty	70	vard	Varied
39	Fn	Fine		54	glac	Glacial	71	uneu	Uneven
40	crs	Coarse		55	ten	Tenacious	(Sl)	S/M	Surface layer and Under layer
41	sft	Soft		56	wh	White			
42	hrd	Hard		57	bk	Black	76		Freshwater springs in seabed
43	sml	Small		58	vi	Violet	(Sd)	/\/\/	Mobile bottom (sand waves)
44				59	bu	Blue			

T. Tides and Currents

1	HW	High water		17	Str.	Stream
1a	HHW	Higher high water		18		Current; general, with rate
2	LW	Low water		19		Flood stream (current) with rate
2a	LLW	Lower low water		20		Ebb stream (current) with rate
3 (Ta)	LWD	Low-water datum		21		Tide gauge, Tidepole; Automatic tide gauge
3a	LLW	Lower low water		23	vel	Velocity; Rate
4	MTL	Mean tide level		24	kn	Knots
4a	MSL	Mean sea level		25	ht	Height
4a		Elevation of mean sea level above chart (sounding) datum		26		Tide
4b		Chart datum (datum for sounding reduction)		27		New moon
5	Sp	Spring tide		28		Full moon
6	Np	Neap tide		29		Ordinary
7	MHW	Mean high water		30	Sp	Spring
8	MHWS	Mean high-water springs		31		Neap
8a	MHWN	Mean high-water neaps		33		Total stream diagram
8b	MHHW	Mean higher high water		34		Place for which tabulated tidal stream data are given
9	MLW	Mean low water		35		Range (of tide)
9a	MLWS	Mean low-water springs		(Tb)		Phase lag
9b	MLWN	Mean low-water neaps		(Th)		Current diagram, with explanatory note
10	MLLW	Mean lower low water				
11	ISLW	Indian spring low water				
11	HW F&C	High-water full and change (vulgar establishment of the port)		1(Tx)	CRD	Columbia River Datum
12	LWF&C	Low-water full and change		1(Ta)	GCLWD	Gulf Coast Low Water Datum
13		Establishment of the port				
14		Unit of height				
15		Equinoctial				
16		Quarter; Quadrature				

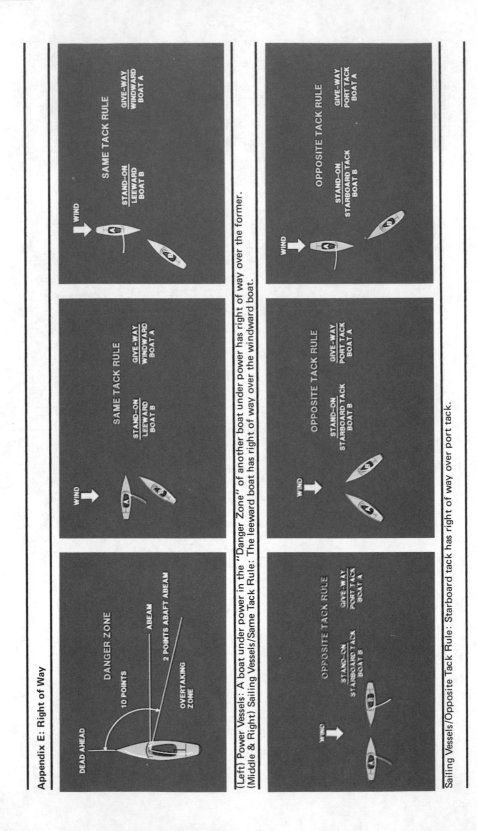

(Left) Power Vessels: A boat under power in the "Danger Zone" of another boat under power has right of way over the former.
(Middle & Right) Sailing Vessels/Same Tack Rule: The leeward boat has right of way over the windward boat.

Sailing Vessels/Opposite Tack Rule: Starboard tack has right of way over port tack.

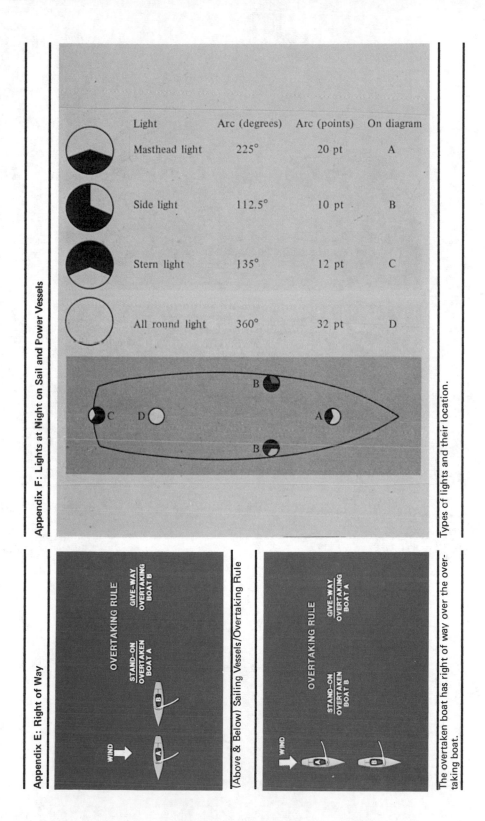

Appendix F: Lights at Night on Sail and Power Vessels

Light	Arc (degrees)	Arc (points)	On diagram
Masthead light	225°	20 pt	A
Side light	112.5°	10 pt	B
Stern light	135°	12 pt	C
All round light	360°	32 pt	D

Types of lights and their location.

Appendix E: Right of Way

OVERTAKING RULE

STAND-ON
OVERTAKEN
BOAT A

GIVE-WAY
OVERTAKING
BOAT B

WIND

(Above & Below) Sailing Vessels/Overtaking Rule

OVERTAKING RULE

STAND-ON
OVERTAKEN
BOAT B

GIVE-WAY
OVERTAKING
BOAT A

WIND

The overtaken boat has right of way over the over-taking boat.

Appendix F: Lights at Night on Sail and Power Vessels

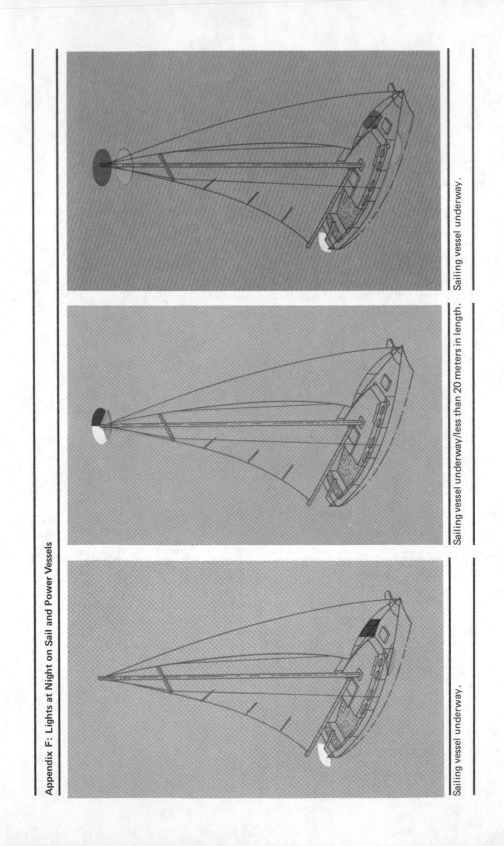

Sailing vessel underway.

Sailing vessel underway/less than 20 meters in length.

Sailing vessel underway.

Appendix F: Lights at Night on Sail and Power Vessels

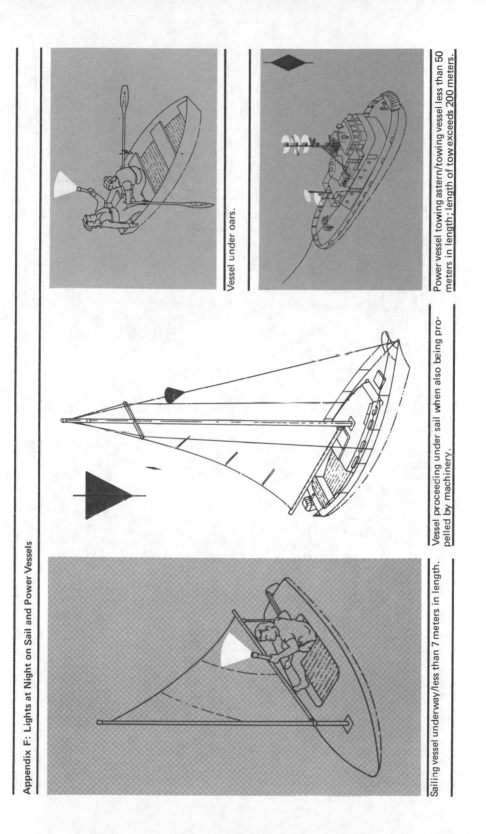

Vessel under oars.

Power vessel towing astern/towing vessel less than 50 meters in length; length of tow exceeds 200 meters.

Vessel proceeding under sail when also being propelled by machinery.

Sailing vessel underway/less than 7 meters in length.

Appendix F: Lights at Night on Sail and Power Vessels

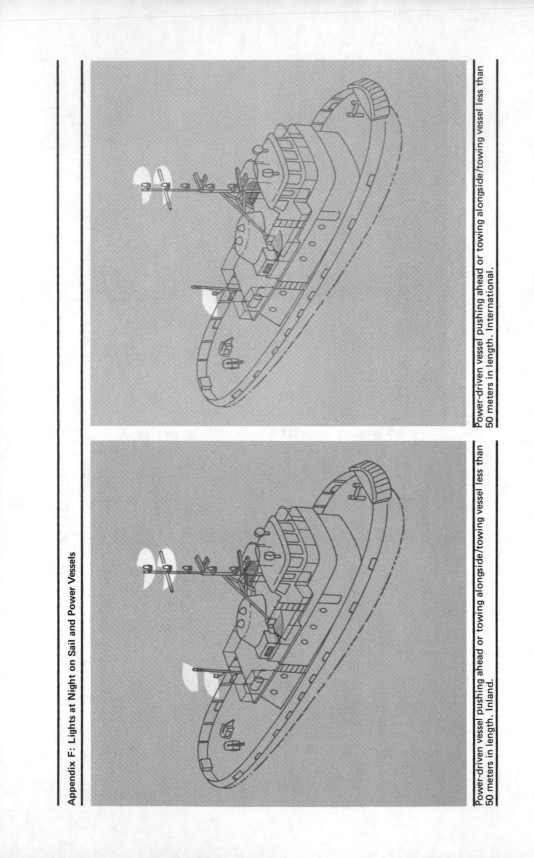

Power-driven vessel pushing ahead or towing alongside/towing vessel less than 50 meters in length. Inland.

Power-driven vessel pushing ahead or towing alongside/towing vessel less than 50 meters in length. International.

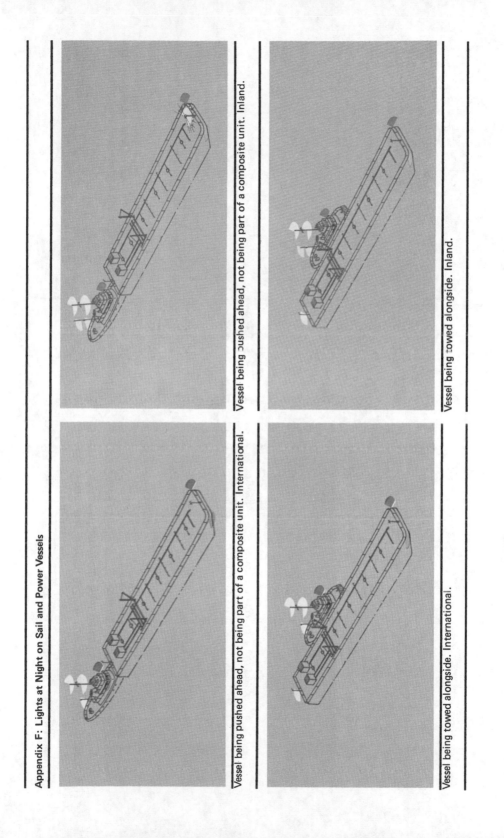

Appendix F: Lights at Night on Sail and Power Vessels

Vessel being pushed ahead, not being part of a composite unit. International.

Vessel being pushed ahead, not being part of a composite unit. Inland.

Vessel being towed alongside. International.

Vessel being towed alongside. Inland.

Appendix G: Sound Signals

Signal:	Situation:	Example:	Meaning:
One short blast	International—vessels in sight of one another under power		"I am altering my course to starboard"
	Inland—vessels under power, in sight or crossing within ½ mile		"I intend to leave you on my port side"
Two short blasts	International—same as above		"I am altering my course to port"
	Inland—same as above		"I intend to leave you on my starboard side"
Three short blasts	International—vessels in sight of one another under power		"I am operating astern propulsion"
Two long, one short	International—in sight in narrow channel		"I intend to overtake you on your starboard side"
Two long, two short	International—in sight in narrow channel		"I intend to overtake you on your port side"
One long, one short, one long, one short	International—in sight in narrow channel		"I agree with your signaled intentions"
Five short blasts	International/Inland—vessels in sight of one another		"I don't understand your intentions" or "I don't think you are taking sufficient action to avoid a collision"
One prolonged blast	Inland—vessel at dock		"I am leaving my berth"

Signal:	Situation:
One long blast every two minutes	International/Inland—restricted visibility, power vessel making way through the water
Two long blasts every two minutes (not more than two seconds between blasts)	International/Inland—restricted visibility, power vessel underway but stopped and making no way through the water
One long, two short blasts every two minutes	International/Inland—restricted visibility: a) vessel constrained by draft b) sailing vessel c) vessel towing d) vessel restricted in ability to maneuver
One long, three short blasts	International/Inland—restricted visibility signals from last vessel in a tow
Bell rung rapidly for five seconds every minute	International/Inland—restricted visibility vessel at anchor
One short, one long, one short	International/Inland—restricted visibility vessel at anchor warning another of her position